YE MARY FORTUNE

Ye Mary Fortune

A Ship of King Henry VII
1490 AD

Pembroke Castle's Link with the Sea

David James

The model of Ye Mary Fortune is displayed in Pembroke Museum in Pembroke town.

First published in 2018

Published with the financial support
of the Welsh Books Council

ISBN: 978-1-84524-273-2

Cover design: Eleri Owen

Published by Gwasg Carreg Gwalch,
12 Iard yr Orsaf, Llanrwst, Wales LL26 0EH
tel: 01492 642031
email: books@carreg-gwalch.cymru
website: www.carreg-gwalch.cymru

Acknowledgements

To My Dear Wife Margaret,
and to the many people who have given their time and effort
in assisting me in this work, whether by offering advice,
allowing me to read and use some of their work,
proofreading and assessing this book's content, or supporting
me when I ran into seemingly unsurmountable snags.
There are too many people to name, but I hope that they all
understand I appreciate the support and guidance they have
unstintingly given.

I keep six honest serving men,
They taught me all I know
Their names are
Who and What and When,
Where and Why and How

Rudyard Kipling

Contents

Introduction

In 2002, a new theatre and arts centre was being built in Newport, Gwent. Builders began to dig down inside a steel coffer dam to prepare for the orchestra pit, under the watchful eyes of members from the Glamorgan-Gwent Archaeological Trust. Quite near the surface, a quay with a cobbled surface and timber drains was discovered, dating from the eighteenth or early nineteenth century. However, the real treasure was discovered only when this was removed. Large timbers appeared, suggesting that a big ship lay hidden; and, as digging continued, with excitement mounting, more and more of her was revealed. Finally, there she was, lying in a tidal inlet which had silted up, presumably after the quay above had been abandoned.

A book published by the Friends of the Newport Ship explains the significance of the find, and the importance of conclusions drawn from examination of the artefacts discovered inside. It confirms that the ship was of clinker construction, which means that each plank in the hull overlaps and is secured to the one below it. This is a style of construction developed mainly by the northern European peoples, particularly the Vikings. A clinker-built boat has to be built outer shell first, with the frames and deck beams being inserted afterwards, a method of construction that requires great skill from shipwrights.

As the Newport ship was dismantled, the stem (bow) post was lifted off the keel, revealing a mortice and tenon joint. In the bottom of the mortice a small recess was found containing a French coin from the Dauphine district of south-eastern France, dated 1446. A few other coins were also found, including four Portuguese and one Nuremberg jetton (a sort of gaming counter). Other evidence suggests she was abandoned in her muddy creek around 1465 or 1466. Clinker-built ships were, at this time, giving way to the carvel construction method, in which a skeleton of frames is erected, and the hull planks fastened to them rather than an adjoining plank. The ships of the Hanseatic League, sailing out of ports on the North Sea coast of what is now Germany, developed this method of shipbuilding. It was quicker and a little easier, but more importantly it enabled larger ships to be built with the added benefit of easier repairs when needed. Due to the stern rudder and greater size of such ships, they also possessed a greater capacity to carry cargo, as well as a military advantage.

Focussing on the Newport ship, what else did archaeologists establish? Her length is about ninety-eight feet (thirty metres), and her beam of twenty-six feet (eight metres) gives a length-to-breadth ratio of 3.75:1. This means she was probably not a very fast sailing vessel, but nonetheless very safe, with a cargo capacity between 150 and 300 tons. The strake (plank) dimensions were 9.8 to 13.1 feet (three to four metres) long x 7.8 inches (200 mm) wide. Also found were stone shot 2½, 3½ and four inches in diameter, as well as a leather valve from her bilge pump. Dozens of wooden barrel staves and heads were in and around the ship, with one of these having an incised owner's mark. It is thought that this mark was that of Robert Baron, a merchant of Bristol who is known to have imported iron from Spain in the 1460s. Another interesting find was a crudely cut door in the side of the ship which caused me some thought. Could this have been a sally port used when she was in service, and if so, what could it have been used for?

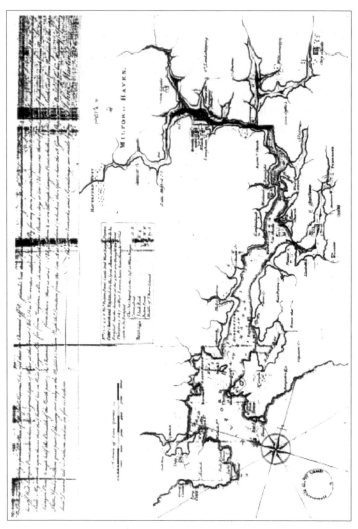

Above is an early print of the Milford Haven Waterway; the 'modern' towns of Milford Haven and Pembroke Dock are not shown. The script above refers to a "28 gun ship being built for his Majestie at Neyland". This was the frigate Guadeloupe ordered in September 1757 to be built by Williams of Milford Haven. After the builder went bankrupt, she was transferred to Plymouth. While this ship was much later than those considered in this book, she does date the map, which gives us an idea of how the Milford Haven Waterway looked before the age of industrialisation.

photo courtesy of Haverfordwest Library

Sources: *Newport Medieval Ship, A Guide*
Edited by Bob Trett
Published by the Friends of the Newport Ship

Aims and objectives of this study

The first aim is to find which construction and rigging details may have been in fashion in the mid to late fifteenth century, including hull shapes, stern and forecastle developments, masts, spars, sails, ornamentation, weapons, and figureheads, etc. This book is also intended as a prelude to a working drawing which will lead to the construction of a scale model of the Newport ship itself.

Chapter one
Mediaeval ship types, construction methods and contemporary history

As the Newport ship had a French coin built into her, this raises the question of whether she was built in a southern European shipyard. Considered are the Northern ship types, but we must also look at the Southern European ones, seeking various construction methods for comparisons and converging construction styles. Clinker construction was practised on the Atlantic coast of Europe as far south as northern Portugal (southern Portugal had been occupied by the Moorish Almohad dynasty, who were finally driven out of southern Iberia in the late fifteenth century).

Coins found loose in the wreck included four Portuguese and one Nuremberg jetton, while built into ship was one French coin from the Dauphine district of south-eastern France, dated 1446. Thus, since no northern European coins were found, could she have been built in Portugal? This idea is merely suggested as no northern European coins were found aboard. Could she perhaps have been taken in a skirmish at sea and brought to Newport as a prize, or was she trading between England and France and just happened to end her days in Newport?

Sources: *Cogs, Caravels and Galleons*
             Edited by Robert Gardiner & Richard W. Unger
             Published by Conway Maritime Press

             Newport Medieval Ship, A Guide
             Edited by Bob Trett
             Published by the Friends of the Newport Ship

Contemporary quotations

Your great ship the Grace Dieu is ever as ready and is the fairest that ever men saw.
Humphrey, Duke of Gloucester, to Henry V, c. 1420

Hale how well and rumbylowe,
Steer well and let the wind blow
Red Book of Bristol, fifteenth century

O see how well our good ship sails
'The Pilgrims Sea Voyage', fifteenth century

Evidence sources

Much is known about Viking and Saxon ships from finds such as the splendid Oseberg and Gokstad ships, and those scuttled in the Roskilde bay in Denmark, as well as the Saxon ship found at Sutton Hoo in eastern England. Plans of vessels of the Middle Ages do not exist; shipwrights of the time worked to the *'rule of thumb'* formulae they learnt as apprentices while building boats and ships. Thus, pictorial evidence is confined to manuscripts, church carvings, tapestries and town seals. While these are valuable sources of information, they are never to scale, and the construction details often have deliberate omissions. If town seals, for example, were to correctly show every rope, it would result in a meaningless tangle in such a small circle. Mindful of this, I have tried to find images made in the fourteenth, fifteenth and early sixteenth centuries. Comparing those found, and keeping them in chronological order, discovering the common denominators and differences between northern and southern European ship design and construction, has revealed some facts.

The English merchant fleets of the 1450s contained

some large ships, many of 300 to 400 tons. After this period, there was a decline, and ships so large were not built again until the early seventeenth century. However, some ships from southern France and Brittany of the same period were very large, with five recorded as being of 800 tons, and one of no less than 1,000 tons. This decline in ship size coincides with the great change in direction of shipbuilding techniques away from the clinker-built method, in which the shell of the ship was built first, and the frames and deck beams inserted later. Such construction methods in larger ships became difficult and repairs extremely so.

The succeeding method was to build a skeleton of frames first and then plank the outside of the standing frames. This was a cheaper method of construction, leading to the creation of large numbers of smaller merchant ships, easier to repair and suited to tiny mediaeval harbours. A few Royal great ships were still built, but by around 1500 to 1510, the carvel-built ships had replaced the clinker-built one completely.

In late July 1545, some German clinker-built ships of 400 and 500 tons were arrested for Royal service and taken to Portsmouth to assess their suitability for use in the Royal fleet. The Lord High Admiral rather contemptuously dismissed them with the remark, "They are clenchers, both feeble, olde and out of fashion."

Shipbuilding
Noah is the only Biblical shipbuilder, and so he became the symbol of mediaeval shipwrights. There are numerous images detailing the construction of the Ark, often with Noah hard at work or pausing to hear God's words. This theme was naturally adopted by the shipwrights themselves, and they put on Corpus Christi plays which included the building of the Ark. These were performed in York from

1376 and Newcastle upon Tyne from 1427. In Bristol in 1486, a lavish pageant was performed for the new King, Henry VII, and in one of the speeches it was lamented that "Bristow is fallen into decay" through ship losses and other troubles. They implored Henry to restore the local shipping and cloth industries. It continued with, "The Shipwrights pageaunt, with praty conceyt splaying in the same without any speche."

Moved by this, Henry agreed to encourage Bristol's trade and shipping. Shipwrights guilds existed in Newcastle, York, London and elsewhere; but the trade was poorly organised and did not have the economic influence of other mediaeval guilds. The London guild was the fraternity of St Jude and St Simon; both saints appear in images on manuscripts holding boats recorded as early as the late 1360s. The earliest set of ordinances for this guild date from 1426, with some amendments in 1483. These outline the internal organisation of the guild, apprenticeships and the importance of ensuring a good standard of workmanship.

Between 1428 and 1443, six London shipwrights were recorded in the city records as being sworn in as masters of the "mistery of shipwryghtis", but unfortunately most early records seem to have been lost in a fire. At the time, there were no naval shipyards, with construction focussing on merchant ships that could be converted to a military use in times of war. There were some shipyards used to repair Royal ships, but these were rather short lived; the foundation of what would later become Portsmouth Dockyard would not be laid until 1495. Henry VIII finally prompted the growth of shipyards at Deptford, Woolwich and Erith in the early years of the sixteenth century, and set off the beginning of the London shipbuilding industry. However, even in the late 1500s, master shipwrights were building more merchant ships than warships.

Between 1200 and 1520, the shipbuilding industry seems to have had relatively small numbers of men, with it offering a not very respected profession and supplying little corporate organisation, though within the shipyards themselves, organisation was good and remained consistent for 150 years. The *Grace Dieu* of 1418 was one of the largest ships in Europe at the time, which was an astonishing achievement for the small number of shipwrights that worked on her. In view of this, English shipwrights appear to have been the equal of their continental competitors. Despite the great leaps forward in technology of the time, mediaeval shipyards were rather makeshift and ramshackle places. The ground that the ships were being built on soon became muddy and littered with unusable wood shavings and chips, and the smoky air smelt of pitch and tallow. On some sites, partially excavated docks degenerated into holes in the ground which filled up with water, becoming a hazard for the unwary.

The lack of industrial organisation may have had its benefits, as a better organised industry with a strong guild may have resisted the demands for change, particularly when it became obvious that the clinker construction method of shipbuilding had reached its peak. English shipwrights seem to have adopted the new system without too much difficulty.

Sources: *The Good Ship*
              Written by Ian Friel
              Published by the British Museum Press

Logistics of men & horses
Mediaeval armies depended upon a continuous supply of materials which were taken to towns for transportation to Channel ports. They would then be sent on to France, thus

enabling troops to keep up the momentum of whatever war was being fought at the time. This was particularly evident during the Hundred Years' War, when English troops repeatedly invaded France using cogs, which required very little adaptation.

Modification of the cog merely meant constructing stalls in the holds for the knights' warhorses or destriers, of which a great many were ferried across the Channel between 1338 and 1339, having originated from a few southern counties. Hundreds of wooden tuns to carry water for the horses were made, as well as 16,000 wooden hurdles to separate the horses, and 200 gangways were constructed and taken to the embarkation ports of Southampton, Portsmouth and Plymouth. For the King's expedition of 1359, no less than 3,245 horses were shipped from Sandwich to Calais. Remarkably, after the campaign, 6,313 horses were brought back! As the sea voyage was short, a shuttle service was organised to transport all the men, horses, supplies and weapons.

Horses were put in individual stalls to ensure they came to no harm in rough seas. Food and water for the horses had to be carried in addition to all the other military supplies brought aboard. Transport by ship presented administrative problems, as compensation had been promised for every horse lost or killed during the campaign. Each animal was examined by a military leader and a Royal official who assessed its condition at embarkation.

Loading horses into a high-sided ship presented difficulties, particularly in cogs; horses could not easily be loaded onto the upper deck without quays of the correct height, after which they would be lowered into the holds, particularly if large numbers were to be embarked. To solve this problem, holes were cut in the side of a ship and long gangways placed by the hole. Some gangplanks were thirty feet (9.1 metres) in length and five feet (1.5 metres) wide, but most were fifteen to twenty feet (4.5 to 6.1 metres) long. Ideally, every knight had four horses, each squire three, and mounted archers two; so, the enormity of the logistical problem becomes apparent.

Several methods of loading horses were tried, but the most efficient was to provide ships with suitable gangways. Hurdles of about seven feet (2.1 metres) x four feet (1.2 metres) were used to form a stall for each horse, keeping them separate from each other. Boards, ropes, nails, wooden tuns, canvas and metal rings were all used for this purpose. Such ship modifications were necessary if horses were to be transported without causing undue stress or physical strain to them, and to meet their dietary needs, which was essential if they were to arrive at the battlefield in excellent condition.

A thought – the images shown in this chapter all have the sally ports open (i.e. not closed by a shutter or door), and they are illustrated in relatively calm waters. If a ship was to make several Channel crossings transporting horses, it is highly likely that the ammonia generated from animal urine would make conditions below decks unbearable, requiring the hold to be ventilated by any means possible.

Battle of Sluis, 1340

Assembling a fleet, modifying ships, impressing sailors to crew them, and loading men, horses and military supplies – all of this was of little use if the English did not have command of the English Channel. After war broke out in 1337, English coastal towns had a great fear of raids by French forces and even of an invasion. Between 1338 and 1339, ports along the south coast were raided, with Sandwich, Hastings and Portsmouth partially burnt, while Folkestone, Dover, Thanet and the Isle of Wight were harassed, and even Southampton was damaged. Many ships were lost during these raids and trade was badly affected. King Philip VI of France planned a major invasion of England in 1339, but his fleet was scattered by a storm.

Edward III responded by commanding an English fleet against a combined French, Castilian and Genoese fleet at Sluis the following year and winning a decisive victory. This was the greatest victory of the war and the most decisive one, coming a full six years before Crécy, where the longbow wreaked havoc among the French army. Thus, the Battle of Sluis was a pivotal point, with Edward leading the battle from his flagship against a numerically superior fleet. If the English had lost that day, the French would have been free to command the English Channel and possibly even prepare for an invasion. Importantly, the victory enabled the English fleet to transport military supplies across to France unhindered.

Another hazard arose when merchants decided to become pirates or suffered piracy; in the former case, they would usually offer the excuse that the ship they attacked was an enemy of their country! Truces were conveniently forgotten and suits to the Crown were often the only recourse. These appeals survive as the record of such actions on the high seas. They were crimes of convenience and a poor excuse to justify the plunder of someone else's ships.

The Admiralty tried on occasions to patrol the Channel coasts but it's effectiveness in suppressing piracy is not known. The fourteenth-century 'merchant venturers' may have been discouraged, but the large profits to be made were worth the risk. The only effective deterrent to such high seas piracy was to adopt the convoy system, which happened at some point in the late thirteenth or early fourteenth century. Convoys were particularly successful in the English wine trade to Gascony, while larger fleets of merchantmen were escorted by Royal ships filled with men-at-arms able to fight off individual ships or even small pirate fleets. Transport ships were assigned detachments of armed men and archers to provide defence against attack. It was in the crew's interest to join in the fighting and so the pirates must have faced a military force determined to thwart their plans. Crews were not paid wages at this time but were entitled to a share of the net profit when cargo was delivered safely and sold. Thus, if a ship's cargo was lost through piracy, the crew could not expect any remuneration, even if they had been at sea for many weeks.

The wine transports trading with Bordeaux regularly travelled in convoy to protect themselves against French and Castilian men-of-war and pirates. The threat was strong enough to persuade the English ships to arm themselves and seek safety in numbers. However, some merchants were not willing to endure the cumbersome and time-consuming rigmarole involved in convoy formation, nor to then follow a prescribed route to Bordeaux, instead preferring to take a chance on avoiding the French or Castilian merchants cum pirates by way of the high seas. The same could be said of the French and Castilian merchants, but they were not so much dependent on seaborne trade as the English wool exports and wine imports.

The cross-Channel English wine and wool trade was a major source of income to the English economy. Seaborne commerce was also a source of income for the Crown, as customs records show. The decline in trade was a serious threat to the English economy, and to Crown revenue, which became a serious matter directly affecting King Edward's ability to wage war. Thus, it was essential that he seized control of the English Channel if he was to be able to trade and to transport his army in times of war. In about 1340, the English were reputed to be masters of the Channel, but the French and their allies frequently retaliated by raiding English coastal ports, and the attacks on merchant convoys in the Bay of Biscay continued unabated.

In the 1340s, large fleets were assembled and sent against the French coasts, but this did not require total command of the sea, as the French mustered equally large flotillas of several hundred ships to intercept the English expeditions of 1342 to 1343. The victories in the land battles of Crécy in 1346 and Poitiers in 1356 tend to mask the major logistical achievements required to transport the men, horses and military supplies which were needed to successfully wage war on mainland Europe.

As already alluded to, the key to this success was the cog; this was the primary troop transport, fleet auxiliary and warship of the era. While the war at sea was an important factor in the Hundred Years' War, in the age of mounted knights and massed armies, the supply of men and materials to the battlefield was crucial to a successful outcome of any campaign. In all overseas wars the cog was clearly the best bulk carrier of the day, but the French tended to depend on galleys, as these were used in the defence of their coastal towns and harbours.

Cogs were requisitioned when the need arose, and as the English were constantly fighting abroad, cogs were constantly being arrested for Royal service. They ranged from thirty tons to several hundred tons, with each cog being allocated to a task best suited to her individual size. Indeed, these vessels were quickly converted to military use, and once the emergency had passed, just as easily reverted to their bulk-carrier role, conveying the major cargoes of wool and wine. Since the taxes generated by these goods, and the myriad of lesser cargoes, were major generators of Crown revenue, cogs were what kept the wheels of commerce turning, generating income which enabled the war effort to be maintained. The galleys and oared vessels used by the French did not easily lend themselves to the dual role of warship and bulk carrier, and this would explain why the cog was the mainstay of European commerce as well as war.

Sources: *Cogs, Caravels and Galleons*
             Edited by Robert Gardiner & Richard W. Unger
             Published by Conway Maritime Press

Edward III, *Les Espagnols sur Mer*, 29 August 1350

This naval engagement was fought off Winchelsea between Edward's ships and a larger Castilian fleet – allies of the French who were returning home after a trading expedition to Flanders. Edward's son, the chivalrous Black Prince, accompanied him as the English fleet lay in ambush somewhere between Dover and Calais. This was not a 'land-tactic' battle fought at sea, but a genuine naval engagement in which cannon were used at sea for the first time, with ship handling and the strength of ship construction counting as much as the bravery of soldiers. The Iberians had anticipated an attack and loaded stones and iron bars, and built projectile throwers on their decks to bombard English ships. There is also a suggestion that the Castilian vessels were larger than the English ones.

The French writer Jean Froissart records that the Castilian fleet sailed down the Channel with colourful streamers flying. The fleet formation is not recorded but the narrative turns directly to the start of the melee, when Edward's ship (possibly the *Cog Thomas*) decides to joust with a larger Castilian ship, which was bearing down on him with the advantage of a following wind. The King's ship turned to meet her and struck with a mighty crash. They rebounded from the collision, the King's ship withstanding the force of impact because of her sturdy construction. The topcastles of the two ships became entangled and the mast of the Castilian ship snapped off and fell into the sea, killing all the men on her in the process. Edward's ship started to take on water because of the collision, and he decided to grapple and board one of the enemy ships before his own sank under him. The English scrambled aboard into a hail of stones and iron darts but managed to take her, and then threw the defenders into the sea. By this point, daylight was fast fading.

Meanwhile, the Black Prince's ship had been grappled by a big Castilian one, tearing holes in his vessel. The Duke of Lancaster intervened by boarding the Castilian ship from astern, and the Black Prince managed to join him just before his own ship sank. In the chaos of battle, another large Castilian ship moved in and was about to tow away the King's household ship, the *Salle du Roi*. However, one brave soldier leapt aboard the Castilian and slashed the rigging so that she lost way in the water. Other English soldiers followed their comrade aboard and drove the enemy overboard. The other Castilian ships escaped, but between fourteen (Froissart's account) and twenty-six ships (Thomas Walsingham's account) out of the convoy of forty were destroyed or captured.

The battle was a major victory by the English cogs over ships which Froissart writes, "towered over the English" and whose crews hurled heavy objects down onto them. The Black Prince's ship was holed in the engagement but quite how this was done is unclear. The Castilians had used galleys in the Bay of Biscay in the 1370s, and they had been in the English Channel, but Froissart does not mention them in this engagement.

The most important naval engagement when war broke out again was the defeat of an English fleet by the Castilian one at La Rochelle in 1372. The Gascony disaster was complete, with several English ships sunk or captured; many soldiers were drowned, dragged down by their armour. When the news of this defeat reached England, the people were so outraged that increased funding was made available for naval forces. To reinforce the fleet, ten Genoese galleys and one smaller ship were hired in 1373 at a cost of £9,550.

The French relied on ships built in the Royal shipyard at Rouen, the Clos des Gallées, originally constructed by Genoese builders in 1298. Mediterranean-style war galleys were produced there, using southern construction techniques until 1419, when Normandy fell to the English. Before withdrawing from the Clos des Gallées, French forces destroyed the yard and all the ships in the port to prevent the English seizing them.

Despite many victories at sea, King Edward III still regarded his fleet's primary purpose as transporting his armies across the English Channel to fight decisive land battles. Thus, his mediaeval navy was specifically designed to sail in convoy while transporting troops, rather than to be a fighting force. At the time, the English held lands in south-western France, access to which had to be by sea, passing the hostile coasts of Normandy and Brittany. England's main export was wool, which arrived by Calais in the north, with wine being imported to England from Bordeaux in the south-west. Wool convoys sailed regularly, under the command of an official with the ancient title of 'Wafter of the Wool Fleet'. Wine convoys would sail south to Bordeaux in December, load the season's wines and return in January or February.

In 1346, King Edward III assembled a fleet of between 1,000 and 1,100 large ships and 500 smaller vessels in the Solent. After reviewing the fleet, the King embarked from the Isle of Wight on 10 July and sailed the next day accompanied by the Prince of Wales. Their army consisted of many noblemen, 10,000 archers, 4,000 men-at-arms, and a number of Welsh and Irish footmen. The King landed at La Hogue on 12 July and the campaign that followed led to the victory at Crécy on 26 August.

Sources: *Cogs, Caravels and Galleons*
             Edited by Robert Gardiner & Richard W. Unger
             Published by Conway Maritime Press

             An Illustrated History of the Royal Navy
             Written by John Winton
             Published by Salamander Books

Henry V, 1410 to 1422

There is evidence that Henry V constructed clinker-built versions of carracks. Between 1413 and 1420, four great ships were built for the King: *Trinity Royale* (about 450 tons), *Holigost* (about 760 tons), *Jesus* (1000 tons) and *Grace Dieu* (1,400 tons). These were probably the largest vessels ever built in mediaeval England, and the largest in Europe at the time. A poem, the 'Libelle of Englyshe Polycye', gives no doubt as to why these vessels were built:

> Kept than the sea about in special,
> Which of England is the towne wall?
> As though England were likened to a citie
> And the wall environ were the see.
>   Another verse reads –
> It was not Ellis that he caste to be
> Lorde rounde about environ of the see

The poem was supposedly written by Adam de Moleyns, Bishop of Chichester (c. 1436 to 1437). It refers to the defeat and capture of some of the Genoese carracks in 1416. At the time, French and Genoese ships posed a serious threat to English shipping, and both the *Trinity Royale* and the *Holigost* are known to have fought against them. The naval war with France was virtually over by 1420, and so these big ships were laid up. Another *Grace Dieu* would be built as a private venture in 1430, her tonnage unknown. However, she must have been of considerable size as she later came into Royal ownership. An inventory in 1485, shortly before she was broken up, shows her to have been four masted.

As the Hundred Years' War ended, England made her last attempt to dominate by land and sea on both coasts of the '*Narrow Seas*' (the English Channel), a legacy of the Norman Conquest. The population at the time was about four million, insufficient to provide a continuous line of defence, and not even enough to prevent raiding French fleets from capturing and burning English coastal towns. Such acts were feeble reprisals for the much greater amphibious operations launched by the English, such as the invasion of Normandy in 1415. Prior to embarkation, Henry V reviewed his fleet at Southampton on 11 August, probably the first naval review in any modern sense of the term. A few days later, on 19 August, he embarked his army into a fleet of 1,500 vessels, many of which were hired from the Dutch. They sailed with a supposed force of 20,000 common soldiers, 24,000 incomparable English archers, and 6,000 men-at-arms. Crossing the English Channel and entering the Seine River without opposition, they took Harfleur, after which, on St Crispin's Day (25 October 1415), they met and routed a French army at Agincourt. A year later, Henry, not yet master of all Normandy, ordered the laying down of a massive battleship in Southampton, designed to help maintain naval superiority along his lines of communication.

In 1419, a detailed letter was sent to Henry V in an effort to persuade him to buy a large ship being built in Bayonne, and the letter gave some details of her size. She had a keel length of 112 feet (34.1 metres), a main beam of forty-six feet (14 metres) and a stem post of ninety feet (29.3 metres) in height (this may have been measured along the curvature of the stem rather than vertically); and her stern post was forty-eight feet (14.6 metres) high. This suggests the ship was about 1,000 tons burden, almost comparable with the *Grace Dieu* of 1,400 tons. The Southampton ship Grace Dieu of 1,400 tons had launched in 1418. It is uncertain what exactly a mediaeval "tun" represented in modern terms. Despite this, she was certainly the greatest ship to be built in England up until then. Her retinue of two balingers and three cok-boats was built at the same time.

Evidence of the shipwrights is scanty, but one "John Hoggekyn" was employed in 1416 as a master shipwright to work on the *Grace Dieu*. By the time of his appointment, he must have been a man of considerable skill and competence, being paid 8d (about three new pence) per day. In 1492, he was given a pension of 4d per day for physical deterioration suffered while working on the King's ships. This was rather unusual, as most shipwrights were employed on a casual basis.

The *Grace Dieu* must have been a truly enormous vessel as the two balingers, *Falconer* and *Valentine*, were both over 100 tons each. Fitting out seems not to have been completed in time for her to take part in the last great naval engagements of the war, and by 1420 she was in reserve, moored up in the Hamble River with only a maintenance crew of eight men and a quartermaster aboard. In 1434, she left her moorings "in the Rode" for a berth above Bursledon, where on the night of 6 or 7 January she was struck by lightning and burnt out.

An 1859 report about the ship in William White's *Hampshire and Isle of Wight Directory* refers to, "the timbers of an ancient vessel, finely caulked with moss. Its figurehead is a griffin. It was supposed to have been burned by the Saxons". In the 1870s, a man called Crawshay, an enthusiastic antiquarian, used explosives in an excavation which proved be a waste of time, as did several other attempts to identify the wreck. Finally, in 1933, some progress was made when a group of experts including Dr R. C. Anderson; Mr F. C. Prideux Naish and his son; and Michael Prynne, a young Royal Engineer Officer (later Major General), examined her triple-clinker method of planking and correctly deduced that she was the *Grace Dieu*.

Accounts kept by Robert Berd, her Clerk of Works, mention only four guns and a mere 100 pounds of gunpowder. In addition, there were only forty bows issued to the ship on fitting out, which seems rather scanty for such a large vessel. Her main armament would probably have been an infantry battalion, equipped in typical fashion for a combined '*missile and shock*' fight using land tactics on the sea. Once the seizing grapnel had secured the enemy vessel so that it could not break off the action, iron missiles (gads) and stones would be thrown from the tops, helping the archers, whose task was to clear the enemy decks, shooting their arrows so rapidly that a French witness claimed that "it seemed as if it snowed". Once the enemy was decimated and fallen into disarray, the shock troops would board and take the vessel.

As both these manoeuvres required height, the forecastles became a great fighting platform from which to launch arrows and then boarders. It would have been difficult, if not impossible, to hope to attack and successfully board a higher ship, particularly if her defenders were determined and trained. Thus, the larger the ship, the bigger and higher forecastle she could carry, which would itself intimidate the enemy before the engagement began. Such ships bore only a superficial resemblance to the merchant ships pressed into Royal service and modified with hurried forecastles built onto their bows.

Examination of the remains of the *Grace Dieu* have revealed that she had a keel at least 125 feet (38.1 metres) long and a visible beam of some 37.5 feet (11.4 metres). It has been suggested that the actual beam may have been as large as fifty feet. The demands of war put a premium on huge ships, and this explains the need for such large ships, but they were probably useless for any other type of maritime activity.

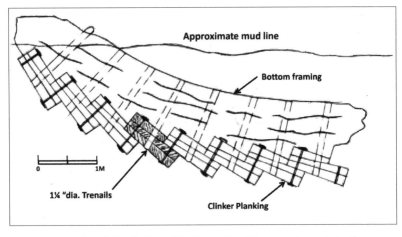

A section through the planking of the Grace Dieu, *this picture demonstrates the unusual triple-skin clinker construction of the lower hull.*

sketch by Maurice Young

Sources: *Cogs, Caravels and Galleons*
            Edited by Robert Gardiner & Richard W. Unger
            Published by Conway Maritime Press

Hampshire and Isle of Wight Directory
Written by William White
Published by Robert Leader

Grace Dieu, 1418
Excavated by nautical experts from the mud of the
Bursledon River, where she had lain since being struck by
lightning and set alight on the night of 6 or 7 January 1434,
the *Grace Dieu* of 1418 is known mainly because of records
kept by dockyard accountants, although these relate more
to costs than ship design. She certainly had at least two
masts, a main and a mizzen; as well as a towering bow
platform (forecastle) and a lower aftercastle. Much of this
detail is gleaned from contemporary town seals. From 1066
to about 1650, there survives, unfortunately, scant
information about ships and their construction.

When Henry V died in 1422, there were over thirty
vessels of 400 to 600 tons, but the Council of Regency for
his only son, the infant Henry VI, sold off almost all the
ships. By 1430, the Royal fleet had only the *Trinity Royal*,
Grace Dieu and *Jesus*, all of which were dismantled, unrigged
and laid up at Bursledon.

Sources: *A History of Seafaring*
             Written by George Bass
             Published by Walker

**John Talbot, Earl of Shrewsbury, killed 17 July 1453 at
Castillon, Gascony**
John Talbot was a Lancastrian noble who loyally served
King Henry VI for many years in Normandy towards the
end of the Hundred Years' War. He spent most of his service
in that province defending Lancastrian interests (and his

own!) against the French King Charles VII. He tried to use the civil war raging between the French dukedoms and Charles VII to prevent them joining forces and becoming a threat to Normandy. Despite his best efforts, there were constant skirmishes against various French forces, with towns and cities in the border regions constantly changing hands. It is recorded that Talbot frequently travelled to and from Normandy and England, even accepting an appointment in Ireland for a year or so. After the fall of Normandy, King Henry VI sent him to Gascony to try to stem the French advances into English-held territories, but his army was exhausted after years of fighting, and finding replacements for troops killed or retired was becoming increasingly difficult. Additionally, plunder was scarce as battles were being fought over lands that had seen decades of conflict, making them wastelands with no or little agriculture, and offering no hope of getting rich by looting conquered towns.

Ships must have played a major role in keeping the armies supplied but little is written about them. However, a little is known about the ships Talbot owned, as after his death it was revealed that he was a merchant as well as a soldier. Unlike most of his peers, he broke with tradition and invested heavily in trade, owning several ships trading in salt, wool and cloth. Four of his ships were disposed of in his will, the *Christopher*, the *Margaret*, the *Carwell*, and the *Tregoe*. A fifth, the *Magdalen Lisle*, returned from Bordeaux after his death. She was loaded with merchandise and handed over to his widow in accordance with his instructions.

His captains occasionally ran into trouble on the high seas. On 16 February 1440, orders were issued for the arrest of Thomas Willamson, master of one of Talbot's balingers for the capture and robbing of a Hanse ship. Two years later, another act of piracy was committed by one of Talbot's balingers when six packs of cloth were taken from a Hanse ship off Queenborough. The goods taken from these acts should be considered as Talbot's profits of war, and thus the actions were legitimate and not out-and-out piracy. It is recorded that he traded in salt from Brittany and goods from Bordeaux. At the time of his death in 1453, he was also a major exporter of wool.

Sources: *John Talbot and the War in France, 1427-1453*
Written by by A. J. Pollard
Published by Pen & Sword Military

Richard Neville, 16th Earl of Warwick, 'the Kingmaker'

In addition to his position as the 16th Earl of Warwick, Richard Neville was also the 5th Earl of Salisbury and Montacute (Montagu), as well as Lord Warden of the Cinque Ports from 1460 to 1471, and Lord High Admiral from 1470 to 1471. Supporting the Yorkist cause in the Wars of the Roses, he was appointed Constable of Calais, which had been captured from France in 1347. This town was of great strategic importance as it held a large standing army and was thus a vital power base during these wars.

In 1457, a French attack on the port of Sandwich triggered fears of an imminent invasion by the French. Warwick was given funding to support his garrison and patrol the English coast. In total disregard of Royal authority, he carried out many acts of piracy against a Castilian fleet in May 1458 and a Hanseatic fleet a few weeks later. He seems to have been a successful diplomat, as he forged good relations with Charles VII of France and Philip the Good of Burgundy. He developed a solid military reputation, and he brought part of his garrison to England to meet up with his father and the Duke of York in the summer of 1459. He was a major influence in the Wars of the Roses, but was killed on 14 April 1471 at the Battle of Barnet, Hertfordshire.

Above is Richard 'the Kingmaker' Neville, 16th Earl of Warwick, 1428 to 1471. This image is from the fifteenth-century Rous Roll by John Rous. The arms shown on Neville's shield are the Montacute arms, and are seen in the second quarter of his own coat of arms.

This is the coat of arms of Richard Neville, 16th Earl of Warwick.
Boutell's Heraldry *confirms that the first quarter of the arms was*
emblazoned on the sails of Warwick's ships, as shown later in this book.

Sources: *Boutell's Heraldry*
              Written by Charles Boutell
              Published by F. Warne Publishers

The demise of clinker construction

One wreck, believed to be Henry VII's *Sovereign* of 600 tons, discovered in Woolwich in 1912, was originally clinker built. Apparently, she was changed to frame construction during a rebuild, as it was discovered that the notches which once fitted her clinker laps had been dubbed away to provide a smooth surface for planks. Nevertheless, a contemporary statement confirms that every effort was made to preserve the ship's hull shape during the rebuild. This information leads us to consider that the drawbacks of clinker construction persuaded shipwrights to adopt the skeleton (frame) first method. Clinker construction lingered on until the 1480s but died out for large ships by 1510. The 800-ton *Great Galley* was probably the last clinker-built warship to be constructed, but she had to be rebuilt in 1523 after deteriorating to the point of becoming dangerous. Sir William Fitzwilliam, Lord High Admiral at the time, said of her that she was the "dangeroust ship under water that ever man sailed in".

It is not known for certain how the skeleton-first (carvel) construction techniques were learned by the mostly illiterate northern European shipwrights. The skills must have been passed from one shipyard to another. Possibly, the shipwrights themselves were itinerant, sailing in the ships they had themselves built. This evolution is perhaps best glimpsed if one considers the word 'carvel', which appears in most northern European languages. This word, in turn, derives from the Portuguese '*caravela*', which was a small, two-masted, lateen-rigged, skeleton-built ship. These were highly manoeuvrable and used by the Portuguese in their great voyages down the African coast. By the 1430s, such vessels began to be seen in northern Europe.

A Caravel, mid 15th Century

The image above is a caravel, mid-fifteenth century. Caravels were said to have been built at Sluys in Flanders from 1438 to 1440, and in 1439 Philip the Good of Burgundy paid some Portuguese shipwrights to build him "*une caravelle*" in the vicinity of Brussels. This seems to suggest that shipwrights travelled when the need arose. A Chancery document refers to a "carvel" in Fowey between 1443 and 1450, while the earliest certain reference is in a Royal grant of protection given on 3 May 1448 to "A certain ship or barge called *Le Carvell of Oporto* in Portugal". This was a ship of at most 80 tons, and the grant permitted the owner to trade with England for one year. The value of such protection was demonstrated a few months later when pirates seized two or three Portuguese caravels off the Isle of Wight. One pirate was the notorious Clais Stephen (possibly of Flemish origin), who is named in a document as master of *Le Carvell of Portsmouth*, which may have been one of the vessels taken in 1448. Just to confuse matters, Stephen is also recorded as the master of the 60-ton *Carvel of Calais*, which was part of the Royal fleet that mustered at Portsmouth in 1449. Hence, it seems certain that at least two caravels were in English possession by 1450.

In 1449, in another act of piracy, a 55-ton caravel from Bermeo, Spain was seized off southern Ireland and taken into the port of Kinsale. Four more were captured in the first half of the 1450s, three of which were Spanish and one Portuguese. Other caravels were legitimately purchased; William, Lord Saye, claimed to have bought his at Sandwich in 1453. Between 1453 and 1466, there was an increase in written references to English-owned caravels, with at least twenty being recorded. Allowing that some may have been recorded twice, this still indicates an increasing desire to own ships of carvel construction. Across the Channel, local records at Dieppe list nineteen caravels brought in for repair between 1451 and 1484.

The French caravel, the *Peter of La Rochelle*, is said to have prompted shipwrights in Danzig (now Gdansk in Poland) to study and adopt the new method of shipbuilding. This occurred despite the Peter being a 600-ton, skeleton-built carrack rather than a true caravel. She was abandoned at Danzig in 1462, where the astute local shipwrights studied her. A Breton named "Julian" is reputed to have taught the technique of constructing caravels to shipwrights in Zeeland in the Netherlands in 1459. Bretons certainly seem to have been active in travelling and teaching this new method of construction. Customs records for Bordeaux demonstrate that Bretons of the time owned numerous caravels.

The first caravel known to have been built in England was Sir John Howard's *Edward* at Dunwich in Suffolk. The first mention is from 10 July 1463, but the actual construction seems to have been carried out between 1465 and 1466 at a cost of £140. Unfortunately, very little is known of her, only that she had three masts.

Sources: *The Good Ship*
Written by Ian Friel
Published by the British Museum Press

Henry VII, 1485 to 1509

Henry VII was the first Tudor monarch, having defeated Richard III at Bosworth Field in 1485, finally bringing the Wars of the Roses to an end. After Henry V's reign, it had become clear that an aggressive military policy on the Continent was unwise, and that the aims of England could be achieved more cheaply by holding the Calais bridgehead, with a fleet strong enough to support it when needed. This led to a general policy of limited land war, enabling the resources of a small nation to be concentrated on the sea, a strategy adopted by the English until the twentieth century.

A period of exhaustion existed after the end of the Hundred Years' War and no large warships were needed or built. In 1487, England began to rearm, and Henry VII invested in two large prestige warships. These were the *Sovereign*, which was probably about 800 tons; and the *Regent*, which was about 1,000 tons, and of which no images exist. They were both carracks (evolved from cogs), with a high overhanging forecastle developed from the old fighting platform, and a lower summer castle aft, which was principally used as officers' accommodation. Such structures were now purpose built and not the tottery cage-work castles '*tacked on*' to a requisitioned vessel. In fact, ships had become strong enough to support many small guns, the muzzles of which poked over the gunwales, with gunports not yet having been invented. Larger and heavier guns were placed lower down in the waist of a ship, again poking over the gunwales.

Huge vessels were the bulk carriers of their day but needed high trading returns or state sponsorship to remain at sea. They also had difficulty in entering and leaving the smaller harbours which made up the majority of ports along European coasts, with these being used as trading posts by smaller and perhaps more cost-efficient ships (less men per ton of cargo transported).

Henry VII recognised the geographic value of Portsmouth as a strategic naval base and improved its fortifications. In 1495, he gave instructions for a graving dock to be dug there – the first dry dock ever known in this country. Thus, Portsmouth began to develop into the naval port we know today. The first ship known to enter the new dock on 25 May 1496 was the 800-ton *Sovereign*, which had been partly built from timber salvaged from the wreck of the *Grace Dieu*. She remained in dock for more than eight months, mainly because there was no pressing need for her services, and it was thought that a ship in dock lasted longer than one afloat. The next ship to be put in the dock was the *Regent*, about 1,000 tons. This time there was pressing naval need for her services, and so she was only in dock from 4 March to 23 April 1497. She was again in Portsmouth on 1 May, and on the 14 May she was the flagship of the Earl of Surrey in the fleet that sailed against James IV of Scotland.

King Henry had the heart and soul of a merchant; he believed in making every penny count and wherever possible making others, especially his nobles, pay the bills. He is credited with laying the foundations of the Royal Navy, and while he did lay down the foundations for the building and repair of ships at Portsmouth, he built few himself, preferring to hire Spanish ships, as their rates were lower. In addition to *Sovereign* and *Regent*, he seems to have built two smaller warships, *Sweepstake* and *Mary Fortune*, each described in the King's inventories as the "Kynges New Barke". They were each three-masted, with a main topmast, a mizzenmast, a spritsail on the bowsprit, and eighty and sixty oars, on *Sweepstake* and *Mary Fortune*, respectively. Both served in 1497 in the fleet under Robert Lord Willoughby de Broke against the Scots.

Bernard Hagendorn, in *Die Entwiklung der Wichtigsten Schiffstypen (The Development of the Most Important Types of Ships until the 19th Century)*, states that orders came from Italians to build ships in Gdansk. That port was presumably chosen for its availability of wood, as well as cargoes for maiden voyages west and south. This suggests that the best ideas and new practices developed by northern and southern shipbuilders were becoming interchangeable around 1489.

The fact that shipping had taken on a general European dimension was already evident in the late fourteenth century. The structure of demand for ships became increasingly similar for all builders. At the same time, technical innovations of the fifteenth century made certain designs significantly superior to earlier ones and made the new forms acceptable for many jobs in many different places. This is not to say regional and local differences were eradicated; however, by the end of the fifteenth century, the pattern of design development had become general throughout Europe. Contact between regions increased too, and English shipbuilders turned themselves to the construction of similar types found in most of the major ports of the Continent. There was still a difference between the types of ships built in northern Europe and those built in the south. Factors which influenced this were the climate, the nature of the winds and tides, and the generally different sailing conditions of the Baltic, North Sea, Atlantic and the Mediterranean. Of course, it was the borrowing and copying of design features which enabled shipbuilders to create a range of highly versatile vessels. Eventually, these vessels, with minor adjustments, could be used anywhere in the world.

Sources: *A History of Seafaring*
              Written by George Bass
              Published by Walker

              Cogs, Caravels and Galleons
              Edited by Robert Gardiner & Richard W. Unger
              Published by Conway Maritime Press

An Illustrated History of the Royal Navy
Written by John Winton
Published by Salamander Books

The Ship in the Mediaeval Economy, 600-1600
Written by Richard W. Unger
Published by McGill-Queen's University Press

Die Entwiklung der Wichtigsten Schiffstypen
Written by Bernhard Hagedorn
Published by Karl Curtius

Henry VIII, 1509 to 1547

The *Sweepstake* was taken into Henry VIII's navy, and was rebuilt in 1511, being renamed *Katherine Pomegranate* in honour of Katherine of Aragon. The pomegranate was in the coat of arms of Granada, the capture of which from the Moors was a victory for Christendom. The pomegranate was also often used as a badge after Katherine of Aragon's arrival in England.

Henry VIII improved land defences with round castles housing artillery, and he also saw the value of an organised navy. With his construction of Southsea and Dover castles, and his founding of the Board of Ordnance, the drive and vision he possessed are quite apparent. He is especially remembered for his great warships, the shape and size of which were determined, for the first time, by the weight and number of ordnance they might be expected to carry and use. Furthermore, the weapons themselves had to able to conform to and meet the tactical demands of day-to-day engagements. From that time onwards, the dominant type of warship has been a floating battery carrying the big guns into battle, but in times of peace having no commercial value.

In 1509, two ships were laid down in Portsmouth, the *Peter Pomegranate* and the *Mary Rose*. The *Peter Pomegranate* was about 400 tons and armed with sixty serpentines (small calibre swivel guns, weighing about 250 pounds). The older *Grace Dieu* and *Regent* had relied mainly on infantry for attack, with the grapnel preventing enemy ships from escaping and allowing archers and spear-throwers to rain arrows and iron gads onto their decks. The small guns of the two older ships may have helped in this, and possibly damaged the enemy topcastles, further exposing their defenders. This tactic was further developed by Henry, so that guns bombarded and splintered the sides of enemy ships, demoralising their crews and allowing archers to find targets before the shock troops boarded.

The *Mary Rose* was a ship specifically designed to meet the battle tactic described above. Laid down in Portsmouth in 1509, she was the state-of-the-art battleship of her day, representing the current land warfare techniques taken to sea. She was designed to mount a weapons system based on the medium calibre siege guns available, which were then the only effective form of artillery. Field artillery of the day was slow, and even the handgun was clumsy and slow firing, and perhaps as dangerous to the gunner as the person he aimed at. The "Trayne of Artillerie" on land was named well, as the guns and supply wagons may have extended over many miles when on the march, and were hardly suitable for a mobile battle because of the short range of the weapons. However, the value of artillery became obvious when laying siege to a fortified town, with it being used to aid the archers, miners and men-at-arms. Guns were also able to batter a section of wall until it collapsed, allowing troops to storm the breach under covering fire from massed archers. The response of defenders to such heavy cannon was to bring a culverin to bear; with its longer range and smaller shot, it was able to harass the siege gunners. In their turn, the besiegers might also bring their own culverins to bear to try to knock out those firing upon them.

As Henry required this complex battle plan to be taken to sea, the *Mary Rose* was designed. She was a four-masted carrack of 600 tons, originally built in 1509, and she proved so successful that an even bigger battleship, the 1000-ton *Henry Grace a Dieu*, otherwise known as the *Great Harry*, was launched in 1514 at Woolwich. In 1536, *Mary Rose* was rebuilt to weigh 700 tons and armed with new cast-bronze, muzzle-loading guns. *Henry Grace a Dieu* was a rebuilt soon after in 1540 and armed with 186 guns. Both ships were now high-charged carracks with overhanging forecastles, and each had four masts carrying a more advanced rig than earlier ships, as well as sterns which were transom rather than the earlier round tucked ones. Their guns were a complex mix of types, with the larger and heavier ones mounted low down in the hull and peering out of the new gunports, which possessed lids. Thus, what in a merchant ship would have been valuable cargo space, was now occupied by rows of guns. Such specialised vessels could not easily be used for anything else but warfare, with their size effectively preventing them from entering the great majority of small harbours dotted along Europe's coasts.

The *Henry Grace a Dieu* was matched by other maritime nations. The French built the *Grand François*; the Portuguese the *Sao João*, which allegedly carried no less than 366 guns; and the Swedish *Elefanten* of 1532 had seventy-one guns, twenty-four of which were bronze. Rulers of the maritime nations followed the dictates of fashion and the need to '*keep up with the neighbours*', building ever larger and more unwieldy ships which could carry more and heavier guns. In the mid-sixteenth century, these were to evolve into lower, faster and more seaworthy ships.

In August 1512, the King himself rode down to Portsmouth to review the twenty-five ships which had been assembled to reinforce Lord Howard, who was already cruising off the coast of Brittany. Howard, with his reinforced fleet, met the French fleet of thirty-nine sail, off Brest on 10 August. During their battle, the *Regent* grappled with "the great carrack of Brest", the *Marie La Cordelière*, which either caught fire after an unplanned gunpowder explosion, or as one account says, "a varlet gunner, being desperate" set fire to the powder. The flames spread rapidly to the *Regent*, which was to leeward, and so both ships were destroyed. Only 120 of the 800 crew aboard the *Regent* were saved, while only twenty survived out of the 1,500 crew of the *Marie La Cordelière*. The next year, 1513, the French assembled a fleet of eleven warships and six galleys in Brest, under the enterprising commander Pregént de Bidoux, with another sixteen ships in various ports in Normandy. They cautiously waited for Howard to attack but he was unable to do so as the galleys had a distinct advantage in the confined waters of Brest's harbour. Eventually, he chose to personally lead an attack, during which he was killed, and the leaderless English fleet withdrew in confusion.

It was, in fact, Henry VIII's loss of the *Regent* which led him to construct the *Henry Grace a Dieu*. Laid down in the Autumn of 1512 and commissioned in 1514, she was of 1,500 tons, with a company of 349 soldiers, 301 sailors and fifty gunners serving over 180 guns. She was reputed to be a good sailing ship, and Admiral Sir William Fitzwilliam reported to the king in 1522 that she sailed as well as any ship in the fleet, "weathering all save the *Mary Rose*". *Henry Grace a Dieu*, was a splendid ship, always associated with

Henry VIII's name and reign. However, she was only one of eighty-five warships which Henry built (forty-six), bought (twenty-six) or acquired as prizes (thirteen). He also built thirteen row barges, making a total of ninety-eight warships in his navy of the day. In 1547, there were 7,780 men in the fleet: 1,885 were soldiers, 5,136 were mariners, and 759 gunners. Henry's interest in guns and gunnery during his reign led to smaller warships, armed with an ever-increasing variety of guns. He had a "pond made and cast" at Deptford which was large enough to take the *Mary Rose*, thereby starting off the yard there. He also founded Woolwich Dockyard, which practically grew up around the *Henry Grace a Dieu*.

Henry introduced and enforced new regulations for the control and manoeuvring of fleets at sea and the discipline of their crews. The Administration of the Navy was changed from the mediaeval method of one official, to a committee known as the Principal Officers of the Navy, with this name later changed to the Navy Board. This system evolved over the centuries into the Admiralty which survives to this day. Henry saw the need for his navy to become a powerful offensive instrument of policy in its own right, rather than a form of transport for the army and ancillary to its needs. Thus, he is more entitled to be called the founder of the Royal Navy than his Father Henry VII. However, for all his energy and pride in his achievements, he had the humiliation of seeing the proudest of his ships sink before his very gaze, in what might have been one of the most dramatic of naval mishaps in all naval history.

Mary Rose was, in 1544, part of Henry VIII's fleet. In alliance with Emperor Charles V of Spain, he was again at war with France and Scotland. Henry himself landed at Calais on 14 July with an army of 30,000 men and besieged

Boulogne, which surrendered on 14 September. In October, Sir Thomas Seymour was appointed Vice Admiral, in command of a fleet to take winter stores to the garrison at Boulogne, which was now besieged by the French. After this, he was to cruise off the French coast to seize or burn any French vessel he encountered. Unfortunately, strong storms blew him off his station and he struggled back to Portsmouth having lost all his boats and two storeships. Henry was furious but accepted Seymour's explanation.

The King of France, Francis I, decided to retaliate by seizing the Isle of Wight and to use it as a base from which to invade the English mainland, first taking Portsmouth and Southampton before advancing on London. He assembled every available warship on the coast of Normandy, and by the spring of 1545 had a fleet of 150 large merchant vessels (*gros vaisseaux ronds*), and sixty oared coasters (*flouins*) under the Admiral of France, Claude d' Annebault. This fleet was further reinforced by two fleets of galleys from the Mediterranean, one under Polin, Baron de la Garde, and the other under Leon Strozzi, Admiral of the Galleys of Rhodes, who was possibly the best galley commander of the day.

King Henry decided that attack was the best form of defence and despatched his fleet, commanded by Lord High Admiral John Dudley, who was Lord Lisle, and would later become Earl of Warwick, Duke of Northumberland and Lady Jane Grey's father-in-law. Dudley was to go on a raid along the French coast; he sailed up the Seine River and exchanged gunfire with the French, but a storm blew up and both sides broke off the action.

The French fleet sailed from Le Havre, Honfleur and other ports on 6 July, carrying an invasion force of more than 30,000 men. King Henry had advance intelligence of this plan and ordered his fleet to Portsmouth with all speed.

He left Greenwich on 12 July and arrived at Portsmouth along with his retinue on 17 July. The English fleet was comprised of some sixty ships, a few smaller craft, and a force of 16,000 men, many of whom were assembled on Southsea Common. The watchword in the fleet that night was 'God save the King', the correct response being 'Long to reign over us'. King Henry had arrived just in time, as the very next day, the 18 July, the French fleet arrived off the Isle of Wight. During the day, d'Annebault brought his entire fleet round St Helen's Point. His ships stretched in a long line from Brading Harbour, along St Helen's Roads to Ryde.

When the French fleet came into view, the English fleet weighed anchor and slowly approached, with some desultory gunfire being exchanged. The English tried to lure the French onto the shallows on the sandspit, which would have put them in range of the town's guns, but d'Annebault saw the trap and would not be drawn. Both sides disengaged when night fell.

The following day, 19 July 1545, the sun rose on a perfect English summer's day. It was slack water and dead calm; the sea was like a sheet of glass. There was not a breath of wind and sails hung slackly on their yards. These were ideal conditions for the French oared galleys, and for an hour they were brilliantly handled, shooting unopposed against the defenceless and stationary English hulls. Eventually, a brisk offshore wind sprang up and the English ships began to weigh anchor. *Mary Rose* was seen to heel a little. She was fully manned and had her gunports open, possibly with the guns already run out, in anticipation of shooting back at the galleys that that had been having things all their own way until then. Her ship's company was at full strength, which meant she was at her maximum draught. As she heeled, the sea poured in through the open ports and she quickly filled and sank. Sir Walter Raleigh, writing some years later, said of the *Mary Rose* that "by a little sway of the ship in casting about, her ports being within sixteen inches of the water, was overset and lost".

Sources: *A History of Seafaring*
            Written by George Bass
            Published by Walker

Chapter two

Northern ships considered

What did fifteenth-century ships look like? Having looked at the political and military history of the period, I next considered what its ships may have looked like. To understand this, I found as many images of ships from the thirteenth, fourteenth and fifteenth centuries that I could. Throughout these periods, northern European ships evolved from the splendid clinker-built ships of the Vikings and Saxons, while those of southern Europe were caravel-built. Thus, to avoid confusion, the two types are kept separate in the text which follows. The situation is also further complicated in that the southern European method of caravel building was, by the fifteenth century, widely adopted in the building yards of northern Europe. So, the Newport ship, being clinker built, was already considered to be obsolescent in her time, although such ships still survived into the early sixteenth century.

When the collected images were brought together, I looked for similarities in construction styles, sail plans and whatever else might arise. This led me to a shortlist of images that, I feel, suggest the most probable design for the Newport ship. After consulting the archaeological appraisals of contemporary ship finds, I then prepared drawings which I hope are a fair representation of a ship of the period.

Above is a misericord carved on the underside of the choir stall seats. This example shows two shipwrights eating a meal on the shore beside the ship they are working on. Dated thirteenth century.
photo by David James, courtesy of the Dean and Chapter of St David's Cathedral

A second misericord showing St Govan en route to Rome. He was entrusted by St David with the task of obtaining a copy of the Justinian Law, to make sure that Mass was celebrated properly in St David's Cathedral. Poor St Govan was a terrible sailor and suffered from seasickness, and so he is portrayed retching over the ship's side while a sailor pats him on the back. The boat is clinker built and the oar is pushed through an oar port in the Viking fashion. Dated thirteenth century.
photo by David James, courtesy of the Dean and Chapter of St David's Cathedral

The town seal of Haverfordwest in 1277 AD. It shows a clinker with clear Viking ancestry, but flimsy forecastles and aftercastles have been built to give added height when engaging in combat.

sketch by David James

photo and model by David James

(Previous page) A scale model of the Haverfordwest ship of 1277, based on the image in the Haverfordwest town seal. The steerboard (side rudder) can clearly be seen, as well as the partly open cargo hold and a Norwegian-style faering (Viking dinghy) is stowed aboard. Faerings are still used in Norway to this day. The word 'steerboard' evolved into the modern 'starboard', meaning the righthand side of a ship. Paradoxically, the steerboard on the model is on the wrong (port) side of the ship. It was fitted thus as this is how it is portrayed on the town seal.

The town seal of Tenby in Pembrokeshire, dated 1399. This shows a clinker-built vessel with an aftercastle and forecastle as well as a fighting top on the masthead. The bowsprit has a seizing grapnel suspended from it. This was used to grapple an enemy ship and hold her while troops fought with longbows, crossbows, pikes and swords. It allowed them to essentially use the same methods of combat employed by forces on land.

sketch by David James

Willem A Cruce's engravings

Kraeck (Flemish for carrack) 1468

In the image above, we see a 1468 *kraek* (Flemish for carrack). She was possibly engraved by Master Willem A Cruce, for the guidance of the Flemish shipwrights who built the thirty ship models, each about twenty-three feet (seven metres) in length, for the marriage of Charles the

Bold of Burgundy to Margaret of York in 1468. The engraving shows a large armed ship sporting two forecastle decks, each with support for an awning above. These could have been used as protection for the crew from falling spars when in action. With a boarding net spread, they would have also made it difficult for attacking forces to board. A long, new deck is seen above the quarterdeck, again with an awning support aft of the mizzenmast.

Shrouds are attached, northern fashion, by deadeyes and lanyards to channels, but no ratlines are shown. Instead, there is a ladder up the mainmast. The barrel aft of the shrouds may be for storage purposes. Between the quarter galleries on the stern runs an open gallery. On the quarterdeck immediately above the barrel, five guns can be seen, with a swivel gun in the mizzen top and the hint of another in the maintop. Both foresail and mizzen have been developed into propelling sails rather than steerage aids.

No less than fourteen shrouds per side are shown supporting the mainmast and a five parrel truss. Also shown is an unusual system of self-adjusting martlets from the top down to the main yard, designed presumably to spread the load through crowsfeet as evenly as possible along the length of the yard, rather than have it concentrated in one place when hoisting. This can also be seen on the mizzen lateen yard. The seizing grapnel suspended below the bowsprit was a weapon, with its method of operation being to sail the ship bow against the enemy one and drop the grapnel into their ship, preventing escape. A chain prevented the grapnel being hacked off by the defenders, enabling the attackers to rain missiles (gads, arrows, stones, gunfire) onto the enemy ship before boarding and fighting hand-to-hand.

Master Willem A Cruce's second image is taken from a tapestry and shows a *kraek* alongside a quay being attacked by armed men. A crowned man in armour receives a fatal wound. Nobles seem to be scrambling aboard, rather ungallantly leaving a lady who seems to be trying to placate the fighting men around her, while another lady in a gown trimmed with ermine seems resigned to an unknown fate. In the top left-hand side, a ship is seen sinking, her stern high in the air as she goes down. This ship also has a sally port into which someone is frantically scrambling, and a roof over the angled timbers above the poop deck, something not seen elsewhere.

Sources: *Cogs, Caravels and Galleons*
            Edited by Robert Gardiner & Richard W. Unger
            Published by Conway Maritime Press

Further images

This late fifteenth-century manuscript shows animals being herded up a gangplank to board a ship. Oddly, the mast seems to have been lifted out of its step and is shown lying at an angle across the ship, thereby suggesting she was small, with a correspondingly light mast that could easily be raised by the crew without the need for a crane.

Some images of the time show horses being hoisted aboard by windlass, while other sources state that animals would have been walked up sloping gangplanks and through loading ports in the sides of high-sided ships.

Ottoman horse transports were special ships with twin stern posts, enabling a loading ramp to be operated between them rather like those found on World War Two landing craft. While this is not a northern European ship, it is ideally suited for the non-tidal waters of the Mediterranean Sea and shows how the Ottoman Turks addressed the problem of moving livestock by sea.

Photo on the right, page 61:
Sources: *Dictionary of Ship Types*
              Written by Alfred Dudzus & Ernst Henriot
              Published by Conway Maritime Press

 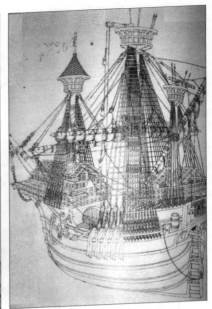

This carving of a three-masted ship can be found in the Hotel Jacques, Bourges, which was built between 1442 and 1451. This is probably the most closely dated depiction of a three-masted, square-rigged ship. The fashion of a lateen sail on the mizzen was not been adopted by this ship, as she still sets a square sail, and the shrouds have been cut short to allow the gunners manning her six guns to be seen. There do not seem to be any gunports, with the guns mounted to fire over the gunwale, but an additional strake is fitted above the muzzles.

This differs only slightly from the *kraek* seen earlier. Interestingly, her shrouds are tightened by lanyards in the southern European fashion, with deadeyes in the northern manner.

15th Century English ship

An early English representation of a ship in the mid-fifteenth century from the Hastings manuscripts. The ship has the characteristically high forecastle of the carrack but her aftercastle is not as high as portrayed in the images of later vessels. The pole on the mainmast may be a topmast or simply a flagstaff. The leadsman is shown plumbing the depth of water

Sources: *Cogs, Caravelles and Galleons*
Edited by Robert Gardiner & Richard W. Unger
Published by Conway Maritime Press

The Danzig Ship C 1400

This single-masted ship is depicted on the seal of Danzig (c. 1400). The through beams are secured with treenails and above them is a stronger wale. Wales have been seen on Mediterranean ships since Classical antiquity, but this is the first time they appear on a northern European ship. Also shown is the ammunition hoist conveying slingshot stones to the fighting top. The triangular deadeyes contrast with the Mediterranean taikle methods of tightening. A vestigial figurehead can also be seen.

Sources: *Sailing Ships*
             Written by Bjorn Landstrom
             Published by Allen & Unwin

Venetian trading galleasse

woodcut by E. Reuwich

The above woodcut was taken from Bernhard von Breydenbach's *Peregrinatio in Terram Sanctam*, published in 1486. It depicts the Venetian trading galleass in which von Breydenbach, the Canon of Mainz, travelled to the Holy Land in 1483. She resembles the *galeazze di mercanzia* which were sailing between Antwerp and Southampton in the first half of the sixteenth century, and which possibly prompted English shipbuilders to experiment with galleasses or oared galleons.

Sources: *Peregrinatio in Terram Sanctam*
Written by Bernhard von Breydenbach
Published by Peter Schöffer the Elder

Oared galley 15th century

Images of galleys in northern European waters are not as common as sailing ships. This image shows a fifteenth-century, ten-oared galley with an aftercastle and a bowsprit but no mast. The oars are in oar ports in the Viking style, with strengthened shear strake. Galleys could move in periods of very calm weather when sailing ships were becalmed, but this advantage was lost as soon as the wind and seas rose, and if their opponent's vessels towered above them.

Willem A Cruce's sketches

Willem A Cruce, who drew the *kraek* seen earlier, also left the sketch opposite; on the foremast is a little furled sail; and a spritsail, to be set under the bowsprit when needed, can also be seen. The majority of images from the fifteenth and sixteenth centuries show the spritsail furled, which suggests it was used in special circumstances to improve manoeuvrability.

The Venetian carrack of 1500 above carries a fourth mast, known as a 'bonaventure'. Also shown are the closely spaced spars of an awning support, which may have been useful in repelling enemy boarders.

Northern European ships drawn by W A Cruce

German ships, c. 1490

German ships circa 1490

Two guns can be seen protruding through circular, unlidded gunports on a lower deck of one ship. An anchor is suspended off the stern of the ship in the centre of the picture, and a small rowing boat has oars through oar ports and is steered by an oar rather than a stern-mounted rudder. The ship on the right has ropes dangling from the bowsprit, suggesting the seizing grapnel has been deployed in battle and lost. One of these can be seen dangling from the ship on the right of the picture.

Sources: *A History of Seafaring*
            Written by George Bass
            Published by Walker

Sail markings

Coat of arms on mainsail of Richard Neville, 16th Earl of Warwick's ship
Boutell's Heraldry

The ships of Richard Neville, Earl of Warwick; Michael Stanhope, Vice Admiral of Suffolk; Louis de Bourbon, Admiral of France; as well as the ship on the seal of Southampton in 1588, all show mainsails decorated with their respective coat of arms. In contrast, Spanish ships carried a simple cross on the mainsail, whereas the Malaga ship had a black sail with a white shield, with five indistinct lozenges in black. A model of a Portuguese ship in the National Maritime Museum Greenwich also shows crosses on all square sails.

Earl of Warwick's ship in battle

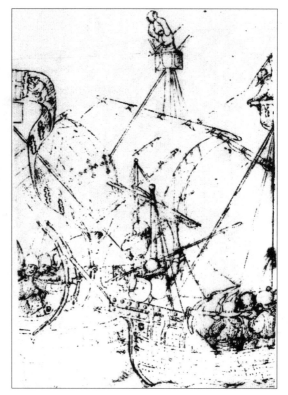

Earl of Warwick's ship in battle

Above, the Earl of Warwick's ship is pictured on the *Warwick Roll* during a fierce sea battle with two French or Genoese ships; his arms can be made out on the sail of his ship, and two large gun muzzles protrude over the gunwale in the waist of the ship.

Curiously, the image on the sail above is the reverse of that seen in the first image, but both are similar. Could the artist have drawn the arms from the front of the ship, while the artist who drew the battle scene showed the sail from the aft? Another of the Earl of Warwick's emblems, the bear and ragged staff, can be seen on his battle pennon flying from the masthead. Longbows and crossbows are seen in action, and a soldier in the maintop has been struck a mortal blow by a quarrel (crossbow bolt) when about to throw a boulder down on the enemy below. Long pikes can also be seen trying to repel boarders.

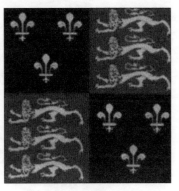

Image of the sail insignia of Henry VII's ship

This mediaeval ship from 1485 clearly shows the coat of arms of the Earl of Warwick on the mainsail, and the ragged staff emblems on the elongated masthead pennon.

Scene from the pageant of Richard

Mediaeval Ship 1485

71

Beauchamp, Earl of Warwick, who was executed about 1485.

Sources: *Sailing Ships of War, 1400-1860*

Written by Frank Howard

Published by Conway Maritime Press

Seal of Louis de Bourbon, Admiral of France 1463–86

Further identification marks

Seal of Southampton 1588

Michael Stanhope ship

taken from the Science Museum, London, 1931

Three-masted ship with square sails on each of the masts; coats of arms are shown on all three sails.

Jasper Tudor's coat of arms, Boutell's Heraldry
(Henry VII's Uncle)

The seal of Michael Stanhope, Vice Admiral of Suffolk, 1493, showing unlidded gunports on the lower deck, while smaller pieces can be seen on the forecastle and quarterdeck. His coat of arms is clearly shown on the mainsail.

taken from Wikipedia

The central motif on the above image closely resembles that on the Michael Stanhope seal, supported by a dragon and a greyhound.

Seal of John Holland, Earl of Huntingdon

Admiral of England, Ireland and Aquitaine, 1436. The sail of the featured ship bears an elaborate coat of arms, filling the entire sail. She also has a pennon of ample size at the masthead. The exaggerated curvature of the planks suggests her method of construction had evolved from hulks rather than cogs. A rudder may be seen at the stern.

Science Museum, London, 1931

1588 town seal of Southampton showing an emblem on the mainsail. It is included to show that this method of identifying a ship was apparently reasonably common.

Sources: *The Ship in the Mediaeval Economy, 600-1600*
            Written by Richard W. Unger
            Published by McGill-Queen's University Press

            Archaeologia Cambrensis, LXXVII (1922)
            Written by Wilfrid J. Hemp, FSA
            Published by Cambrian Archaeological
            Association

The Ark

Mediaeval image of the building of the Ark from *Weltchronik (World History)*, drawn by H. Schedel, 1493. Just below the waist of the ship, four round holes can be seen. These may be gunports.

The Ark
drawn by H. Schedel

Sources: *Dictionary of Ship Types*
Written by Alfred Dudzus & Ernst Henriot
Published by Conway Maritime Press

Schedelsche Weltchronik
Written by Hatmann Schedel
Published by Anton Koberger

King's Lynn pew

A two-masted ship carved on a pew end, formerly in the Chapel of St Nicholas, King's Lynn, c. 1415. She is two-masted, with a square sail on the main and a lateen mizzen sail. Seemingly expecting attack, she has iron gads in the tops, suggesting that the carving may be referring to Henry V's capture of Genoese ships. This hints at the introduction of the lateen mizzen to northern European ships.

Kings Lynn Pew   *15th C men at arms image*

Fifteenth-century men-at-arms

The main armament of fifteenth-century ships consisted of archers and men-at-arms; armoured infantrymen are disembarking from a three-masted ship in the background of the drawing. The ship is four masted and carries heavy guns mounted in the waist to fire through the rails. Gunports are not in evidence.

A four-masted ship from the *Warwick Roll* of 1485, showing three guns mounted in the waist of the ship, above the gunwale (literally the wale over which the guns fired). The term 'gunwale' was first used in connection with Sir John Howard's caravel Edward, of 1465 or 1466. Also portrayed is a long pennant streaming from the masthead.

Sources: *A History of Seafaring*
Written by George Bass
Published by Walker

Santa Caterina do Monte Sinai

Large Portuguese carrack from a painting by C Anthoniszoon (1521) It is probably the *Santa Caterina do Monte Sinai*. Typical example of the floating fortresses of the 16th Century. This ship has no gun ports in the hull but the castles are heavily armed and would be used against enemy boarders in the waist of the ship. Her poor sailing qualities soon gave way to the lower and much more seaworthy race built galleons of Queen Elizabeth I, designed by Matthew Baker

*Santa Caterina do
Monte Sinai*

Sources: *The Galleon*
            Written by Peter Kirsch
            Published by Conway Maritime Press

Louis de Bruges, Lord of Gruythuse, 1482

This manuscript illustration of 1482 shows a ship with guns mounted to fire through circular, unlidded gunports, and more in the forecastle. The manuscript was made for Louis de Bruges, Lord of Gruythuse, whose

*Louis de Bruges, Lord of
Gruythuse 1482*

emblem was a bombard, and can be seen in the margin. Such weapons are still used by armies today, but they are now known as mortars.

Sources: *Cogs, Caravels and Galleons*
Edited by Robert Gardiner & Richard W. Unger
Published by Conway Maritime Press

Passages Outre Mer

Passages Outre Mer 15th C

The naval successor to the cog was the carrack, a vessel that was noted for her extreme size. The image above is from the French manuscript *Passages Outre Mer* of the late fifteenth century. It depicts several carracks with scenes of shipwreck and foundering in the background, emphasising the risks of venturing onto the sea.

1470 to 1480 imitation of Willem A Cruce's work

Ship by Isaac van Meeckeren in the style of Master W A Cruce 1470–80

The ship on the left is by Isaac van Meeckeren, drawn in the style of Willem A Cruce. This little two-masted vessel has a tall mainmast with a top; a small foremast; and a bowsprit, offset to one side of a scimitar-shaped stem post. A row of ports along her side suggest she was pierced for guns, and she also has a series of hoops over the deck. It has been suggested that she is a northern European version of a Portuguese caravel.

Drawings by Hans Holbein, 1530

Drawing by Hans Holbein 1530

A small, three-masted, caravel-built ship. This was drawn by Hans Holbein in 1530, during the Renaissance, and was probably intended to portray Plato's 'Ship of Fools'. Many rigging details have been omitted but those that have been included are well drawn, including a clear representation of a doglike figurehead. She may be a merchantman, as she seems to have only one lidded gunport in the stern.

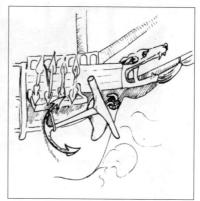

Detail of Holbein's ship showing the figurehead, anchor and shroud.

Holbein figurehead detail

The leadline
This little, three-masted English ship was drawn from a rutter, which is a set of navigation instructions used by sailors to pinpoint their location. The leadline is seen in use, which through a tallow set in a recess in the bottom of the lead weight not only gave the depth of water but the nature of the bottom. The leadline and the hourglass were the

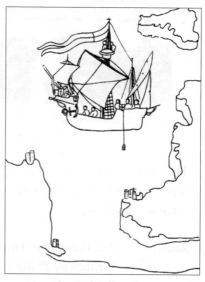

Late 15th century English ship

basic, and perhaps the only, navigational aids available to the mediaeval sailor

Crusader ship from a fifteenth-century manuscript

Crusaders ships from a 15th C manuscript now in Biblotheque Nationale Paris

The forecastle and aftercastle seem to have been superimposed on these ships at some point after their original launching.

Sources: *The Warship in History*
              Written by Philip Cowburn
              Published by Macmillan

Pieter Breughel 1551

Chapter three
Southern European and Mediterranean ships

Vittore Carpaccio circa 1459

Above is a painting from Vittore Carpaccio, c. 1459. It is a detail from the St Ursula Cycle, depicting a three-masted Mediterranean carrack with crow's nest and small topmast.

Replica of Christopher Columbus ship Santa Maria

This replica of Christopher Columbus' *Santa Maria* is included so that comparisons can be made with the ships of northern Europe.

*Picture from the Livros das Armadas, Lisbon Academy of Sciences 1500
taken from Livros das Armadas*

Above are twelve ships of a Portuguese expeditionary fleet under Pedro Alvares Cabral, which departed 9 March 1500, sailing to India on the route discovered by Vasco da Gama. Five of the ships were lost.

Sources: *Dictionary of Ship Types*
Written by Alfred Dudzus & Ernst Henriot
Published by Conway Maritime Press

Livros das Armadas
Written by Anonymous
Published by the Academy of Sciences of Lisbon

Vittore Carpaccio

Carpaccio painting 15th C

In this detail from a Vittore Carpaccio painting from the end of the fifteenth century, he has included a topsail hoisted on the flagstaff of the mainmast and sheeted into the top, which was a new idea at the time.

The Moorish bowl

 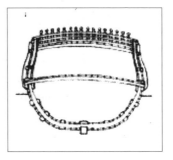

Malaga ship

Possibly the earliest representation of a three-masted, square-rigged ship is found on a Moorish bowl of Spanish origin which was made in Malaga in the early fifteenth century. It depicts a Portuguese ship of essentially the same type as the Mataro model. A new sail, the foresail, can be seen on the forecastle, with this being smaller than the mizzen. Such small sails were used for steering the ship rather than extra propulsion. The mainmast appears to be very thick, and on larger ships it was made up of many spars lashed together.

The shrouds are of southern style, which means they have no ratlines, and a great number of them are portrayed on the bowl itself, as in the *kraek*, but they are not reproduced in the line drawing. Comparison of the pottery image and the line drawing reveals an anomaly: the pottery shows no through beams, but they are clearly shown on the line drawing.

Sources: *Sailing Ships*
          Written by Bjorn Landstrom
          Published by Allen & Unwin

Pizzigano of Venice

Ship by Pizigano of Venice early 14th C

Square-sailed ships needed a mizzen to assist in steering a straight course. The mizzen was a small triangular sail on a mast on the quarterdeck. Pizigano of Venice drew a map in the early fifteenth century and included, as was customary at the time, small ships as well as monsters, whales, mermaids, and winds on the otherwise empty seas.

Ship by Gentile de Fabriano, early 15th Century

This image from Pizigano's painting shows more detail. The yard of the ship is supported by lifts, and the mainsail has a bonnet, which is a strip of sailcloth laced to the foot of the mainsail in light airs. In this image, the crew have been caught out by a squall and the bonnet is tearing free in the rising wind. Also shown is the tiny mizzen, which has been furled onto the yard, together with details of the mizzen sheets. A small boat can be seen towed astern of the ship.

Sources: *Sailing Ships*
Written by Bjorn Landstrom
Published by Allen & Unwin

Model of the Mataro votive ship, Barcelona, fifteenth century

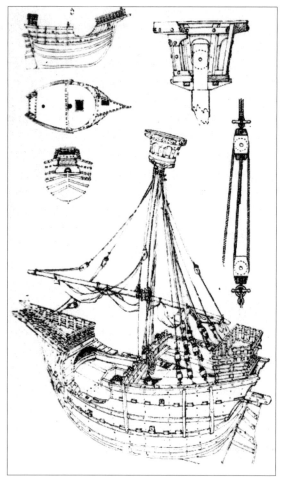

Mataro Ship, Barcelona, mid 15th Century

A seaman's votive model, the only model of the period in which the great voyages of discovery began. She has through beams, even in the quarterdeck, a curved catena under the foredeck, cross and trestle trees under the top, and a triple-parrel truck securing the yard to the mast. On either side of the foredeck is a sheave hole in a clamp, later to develop into a cathead. The model has only one mast but there is a hole in the quarterdeck that suggests she had a mizzenmast. Of particular interest are the vertical, curved, clinker-laid planks under the

Model of the Mataro votive ship, Barcelona 15th C

forecastle, which are such a curious appearance in images of the time. The rigging is in disorder, but the shrouds are clearly tightened in the southern manner, with blocks and lanyards rather than deadeyes.

Sources: *Archaeology of the Boat*
            Written by Basil Greenhill
            Published by A. & C. Black Publishers

            Sailing Ships
            Written by Bjorn Landstrom
            Published by Allen & Unwin

Carracks

Italian Carrack

This Italian engraving is reasonably dated between 1470 and 1480.

This single-masted carrack was redrawn from the Cotton manuscripts of 1445 (British Library, Cotton manuscript Titus A XXVI). The tall forecastle is apparent but the aftercastle is relatively low, and she is without any of the additional structures characteristic of later and larger carracks.

Sources: *Cogs, Caravels and Galleons*
             Edited by Robert Gardiner & Richard W. Unger
             Published by Conway Maritime Press

Deck and hull details by Sandro Botticelli, c. 1445 to 1510

Deck & Hull details by Florentine artist Sandro Botticelli
c1445 /1510

Note the small deck hatches, the capstan abaft the mainmast, and the bitt beam projecting through the hull aft of the foremast. This may have been used to cat the anchor. Note also the very wide planking on the deck.

Sources: *Cogs, Caravels and Galleons*
            Edited by Robert Gardiner & Richard W. Unger
            Published by Conway Maritime Press

Naos

A nao on the cover of the book Libre del
Consolat y del Fets Maritims

This nao appeared on the cover of the Llibre del Consolat y dels Fets Maritims (Book of the Consulate and the Maritime Events). Note the bitts and the curved beam in the deck, to which the anchor cable is bitted.

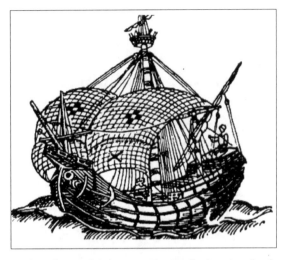

A nao in the chart of Gracioso Benicasa, 1482, which can be found in the library of Bologna University.

Sources: *Llibre del Consolat y dels Fets Maritims*
             Written by Valencian legislators

A single masted carrack redrawn from the MSS of c1445 (British Library, Cotton Ms Titus A XXVI)
The tall fo'cstle is apparent but the aftercastle is relatively low without any additional structures characteristic of later and larger carracks.

Sources: *Cogs Caravelles and*
             Galleons
             Published by
             Conway Maritime
             Press.

Timbotta Manuscript c 1445

Chapter four
Ship details

This chapter is dedicated to considering the size of contemporary ships, and from this attempting to form an idea of the hull construction, rigging, armaments, sail plans and other related details of the Newport ship.

How heavy was the Newport ship?

I wondered whether she was large for her day or just average size, and to explore this I looked at weight calculations and found tables (see Appendices) of ship sizes hired by the English Crown in times of war throughout the fifteenth century. I also consulted the Cotton manuscripts of 1445 (British Library, Cotton manuscript Titus A XXVI) for further information.

Mathew Brown, in 1582, provided information which enabled the calculation formula below to be established. It was later amended in 1669 to a Dutch/Norwegian formula, which was again amended in the eighteenth century, and so:

$$\frac{\text{Length x Beam x Depth in English feet}}{168}$$

Alternatively:

$$\frac{\text{Length x Beam x Depth in metres}}{4.8}$$

The formula states a ship's deadweight and volume in lasts, with the definition of one 'last' being:

- 1.3 tons deadweight of rye (or wheat) in barrels if the ship is open (i.e. with only a halfdeck fore and aft)
- 1.9 tons total deadweight if the ship is completely decked
- 100 English cubic feet
- 1 net registered ton

Applying this formula to the Newport ship, we see:

30 m (Length) X 8 m (Beam) x 4.1 m (Depth in hold)

The length to beam ratio is 3.75:1, with the hold depth having been extrapolated from the Timbotta manuscript table above. Length to beam ratio gives an idea of the stability of a ship. For example, a narrow ship or even a canoe will be very quick in the water but capsize easily; at the other extreme, a ship which is very wide but short in length will be very stable in heavy seas but will be difficult to sail. Thus, the designer must find a compromise between stable and slow, and quick and unstable. The best compromise is usually 3:1, where the beam (breadth of the ship) is one third of her length.

$$\frac{L \times B \times D}{4.8}$$

$$\frac{30 \times 8 \times 4.1}{4.8} \quad \text{gives 205 tons}$$

Comparative sizes of English and foreign ships
The tables in the Appendices are compiled from lists of merchant shipping hired by the Crown for the safekeeping of the sea or to transport troops to the Continent. The

Government agreed to pay ship owners at a set rate per ton, which required all such tonnages to be carefully recorded in the Royal accounts. Records are most frequent during periods of major military operations; two of the longest accounts date from the reigns of Henry IV and Henry V, during the years 1449 to 1450. These relate to expeditions led by Sir Thomas Kyriell and Lord Rivers, respectively, and were attempts to salvage a desperate situation in France. No similar records after the reign of Henry VI have survived, and although both Edward IV and Henry VII engaged in wars on the Continent, nothing from that period exists either.

From the tables, it seems that ships hired by the English Crown did not exceed 400 tons; most were smaller, many considerably so, as were foreign ships granted safe conducts and licences to trade. Southern French and Breton ships seem to have been considerably heavier, with one being recorded as 1,000 tons, with three more at 800 tons. The technology to build such massive vessels existed in England, as the 1,400-ton *Grace Dieu* was built in Southampton in 1418. Other ships of great size include the *Regent* of 1487, the *Jesus* (1,000 tons, built between 1413 and 1420), Henry VII's *Sovereign* of 600 tons, and the undated *Great Galley* of 800 tons. It may be that such large vessels could not use most of the tiny harbours in English ports, or find sufficient bulk cargo to justify their upkeep.

Sources: *English Merchant Shipping, 1460 to 1540*
             Written by Dorothy Burwash
             Published by University of Toronto Press

Construction types and rigging details of contemporary ships

In order to understand the contemporary ship types and methods of construction and rigging I looked at as many images as possible and to find out what they had in common. The details were entered into tables to find the most frequent methods of rigging, gun mountings masts shrouds and the myriad details that need to be established to fully understand the ships of the day.

Thoughts and conclusions from tables

As the Newport ship seems to be of Portuguese construction, I have concentrated on northern European ship types. However, as a coin from the Dauphine district of France (the Gulf of Lyon) was built into the hull, could she have been built on this coast? Intriguingly and coincidentally, the Mataro ship of Barcelona was built in 1450. Barcelona is very close to the Franco-Spanish border, on the other side of which is the Dauphine district. This poses the question of whether the Mataro ship bears any resemblance to the Newport one.

Shrouds

Drawings such as the 1468 *kraek*, 1475 carrack and the *Santo Catarina do Monte Sinai* all show large numbers of shrouds, varying from fourteen to ten per side. Carvings, seal impressions and modern interpretations show far fewer. Is this down to ease of illustration, with the artist omitting detail for clarity? The Hotel Jacques ship of 1445, for example, has the shrouds ending in mid-air, so that the crew may be seen loading the guns mounted to fire over the bulwark in the waist.

Deadeyes

There are twenty-six ship images listed, in which the northern ships invariably used the deadeye and lanyard system of shroud tightening. The deadeyes of the period were triangular, and the method of tensioning remains unchanged to this day, being done by tying the tail end of the lanyard to a sail halyard so that it can be tightened. Once the required degree of tension has been achieved, the lanyard is untied from the sail halyard and made off on the shroud above the deadeye. Southern European ships used taickles, but oddly on the carrack of 1475, both systems seem to be utilised.

Parrels

These varied from a single truck to several securing a yard to a mast, thereby enabling the yard to be rotated around the mast, which allowed the sail to be correctly set to suit prevailing conditions and the desired course. Also, the yard often needed to be lowered partly to enable the crew to reef the sail when the weather deteriorated, with the yard also being lowered to the deck when in port or when a storm-damaged sail needed to be replaced.

On small ships, these 'necklaces' had a single strand of rope with beads strung along it, while on larger vessels, such as the 1468 kraek, a five-parrel truck was used. The 1475 carrack bore three or four truck parrels, whereas other images, when illustrated in sufficient detail, show three truck parrels.

Yards

A horizontal or inclined member beneath which the sail suspended; northern ships usually had a yard made of one piece of timber, whereas southern ones normally had composite yards made from two pieces of timber. However, the images of the 1475 carrack and *Santa Catarina do Monte Sinai* both show two-piece yards, while all other northern images have a one-piece yard.

Halyards

'Halyard' is an abbreviation of the word 'haulyard', which is literally a rope used to haul the yard up the mast. Numerous arrangements of martlets and crowsfeet were employed to spread the heavy loads evenly along the yards, and this is best understood by looking at the rigging diagrams, in which each individual halyard and sheet have been itemised for clarity.

Sheets

The upper edges of sails were secured to the yards, leaving the lower edges loose. To set the sail, these lower edges had to be pulled downwards to fill the sail with wind and provide motive power for the vessel.

Braces

Sailing ships cannot go directly into the eye of the wind; they have to bear away from the wind so that it blows over one side, enabling the ship to move forward. Usually, the ship has to be tacked (turned so the wind blows on the opposite side of the ship) after one hour. This is a complex manoeuvre requiring the coordination of all hands acting on the commands given. Thus, the ship performs a sort of zigzag course, clawing her way in the general direction the crew wish to go.

In mediaeval charts, the wind is often portrayed as a cherub with his cheeks puffed out, hence the expression '*the eye of the wind*'. Braces were the ropes used to pivot the yard round the mast to catch the wind as it blew over one side. Once the order to tack was given, the braces could move the sail to start the ship turning. When through the eye of the wind, the crew would reset the sail in its new position. This had to be done with every sail on the ship, every time the ship was tacked.

Ratlines and mast ladders

Of the twenty-six ships considered, sixteen have ratlines (horizontal ropes making the shrouds into ladders, enabling the crew to go aloft to work on sails). Five other ships have no ratlines but use rope ladders attached to the masts for the same purpose. The two systems seem to have coexisted during the fourteenth century.

Guns and gunports

The first guns taken to sea were mounted to fire over the bulwarks, or gunwales, as they were later called. Heavy guns were mounted in the waist of the ship, which is the lowest point on the upper deck. Smaller guns were mounted on the forecastle and quarterdeck, as well as in the fighting tops. Those in the tops were supplied with ammunition and powder by a crane, clearly illustrated in some contemporary images.

The number of guns in use seems quite low; the 1468 *kraek* has five per side on the quarterdeck and one in a top, while the 1475 carrack has only three per side on the quarterdeck and one in a top. Gunports appear on the seal of Michael Stanhope in 1493, with this showing twelve guns per side, mounted in gunports. The 1490 image of German ships shows two guns mounted on a lower deck protruding through round gunports. The Louis de Bruges picture of 1482 shows six guns in ports, as well as images of bombards mounted on wooden carriages without wheels.

The next development was the installation of gunport lids. These were painted by Holbein in 1530, and featured on Henry VIII's *Mary Rose, Jesus of Lubeck, Grand Mistress* and the *Henri Grace a Dieu*. Notably, the *Mary Rose* was engaging the enemy in a gun battle when she was caught by a gust of wind that caused her to heel a little, allowing water to flood in through her lowest open gunports and sink her.

Seizing grapnel and yard end hooks

Seizing grapnels were attack weapons suspended from long bowsprits; the tactic was to approach an enemy ship at an acute angle. When the bowsprit was above the enemy deck, the grapnel was dropped. Thus, attacker and attacked were locked together. The grapnel was too heavy to be thrown overboard, and being secured by a chain, it could not be cut off. Which ships carried such armaments? Both *kraek* and carrack had them, as did four other ships in the list. Grapnels were in evidence long before the arrival of guns, as sea battles of the time were carried out using land-battle tactics: board the enemy and fight hand-to-hand.

Guns, initially with their short range and slow loading methods, were gradually introduced, and may well have been used to soften up an opponent prior to sending a boarding party over the side. The practice of long-range gun battles was a later development that gained favour in the early sixteenth century.

Yard end hooks were another attacking weapon, used to sever enemy rigging after the seizing grapnel grasped the enemy ship. These prevented the enemy from escape, should they be able to throw the seizing grapnel overboard. Examples of yard end hooks can be seen on three of Henry VIII's ships.

The images of Henry VIII's *Mary Rose* and *Henri Grace a*

Dieu have grapnels suspended on a long bowsprit; they also show grappling hooks on the ends of the yards. The Common Seal of Haverfordwest (c. 1277) shows a seizing grapnel suspended from the bowsprit, and the carrack *Marie Sandwich* captured by the English in 1416 was equipped with a "sesyng grapnell" weighing 370 pounds (168 kg), attached to sixteen fathoms (ninety-six feet, or twenty-nine metres) of chain. Dropping a weight this heavy on a ship's deck could well pierce it, possibly also knocking a hole in the bottom.

Sources: *Cogs, Caravels and Galleons*
Edited by Robert Gardiner & Richard W. Unger
Published by Conway Maritime Press

Hulls and superstructures
Carvel or clinker? Of the twenty-six ships listed, only six have clearly defined clinker hulls. Eleven ships are carvel and the others are indistinct. Many have large horizontal wales to reinforce the sides of their hull, and possibly to provide protection from damage when alongside a stone quay, or when grinding against another ship in combat. Also noticeable are vertical members, sited below the deadeyes to spread the upward pull of the shrouds over as large an area of the hull as possible.

Hull proportions

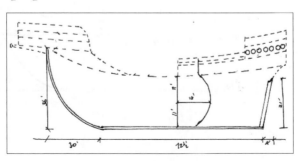

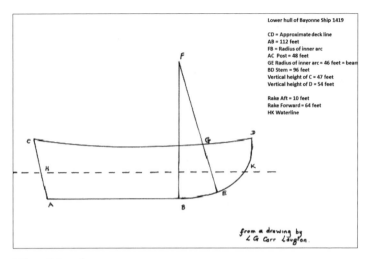

Lower hull of Bayonne Ship 1419

CD = Approximate deck line
AB = 112 feet
FB = Radius of inner arc
AC Post = 48 feet
GE Radius of inner arc = 46 feet = beam
BD Stem = 96 feet
Vertical height of C = 47 feet
Vertical height of D = 54 feet

Rake Aft = 10 feet
Rake Forward = 64 feet
HK Waterline

from a drawing by
L G Carr Laughton.

The ship plans

From the tables seen later, I have drawn on several images to give an idea of the time period's style of construction. The image immediately below (Bayonne ship) dates from 1419, while others are between 1450 and 1485. They all show much of the rigging and hull details so necessary if an accurate model is to be built. The scales and proportions of the images leave much to be desired, but despite this, they do contain a great deal of information.

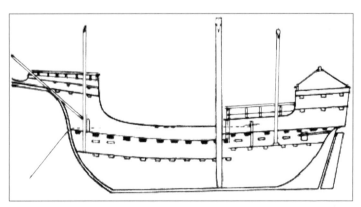

The Bayonne Ship 1419

While this ship is much earlier than the Tudor ship, it is included as a starting point. It should be noted that the awing support over the poop deck is athwartship, in the southern European fashion. See also the *kraek* below:

Kraek 1486

This ship is a detail from the *Warwick Roll* of 1485

The above kraek was drawn by Willem A Cruce in 1486, and could have been afloat at the same time as the Tudor ship. In the image below, we see another view of the Mataro ship of 1450. This model is currently in the Prinz Hendrik Museum in Rotterdam. Portia Takakjian, a noted model shipwright, was given permission to measure this ship model and draw her lines and profile. These measurements were of great help in my preparation of my own drawings, which are shown below.

The Mataro ship of 1450 also described earlier in this work

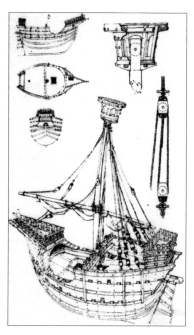

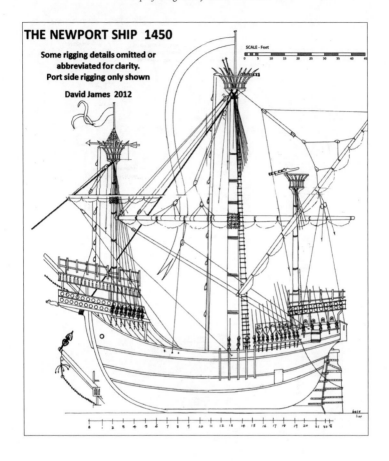

drawings by David James

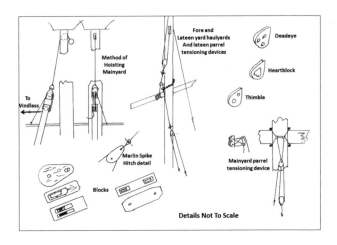

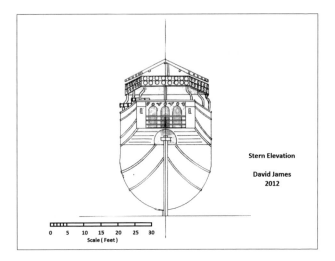

Above are some details of rigging.
Above is the stern view.

drawings by David James

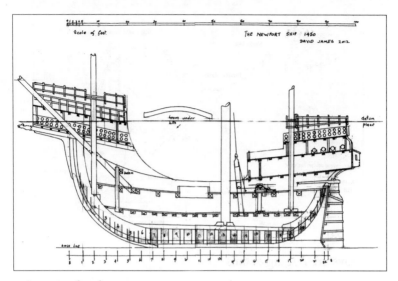

Longitudinal section.

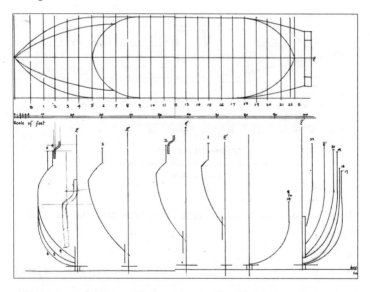

Above are lines and frame jig details. My method of construction is to build each frame and set it into its place in the frame jig. This holds it in place until all the frames are erected prior to planking the hull.

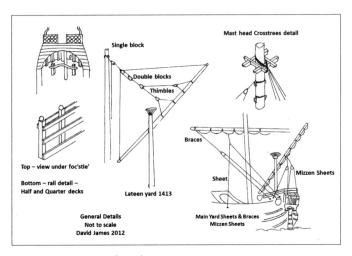

Above are rigging details.

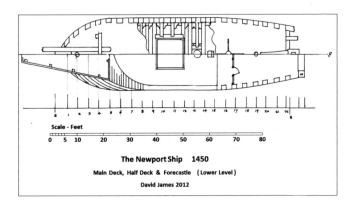

Above is the main deck, with forecastle and halfdeck also shown.

drawings by David James

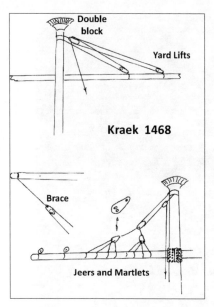

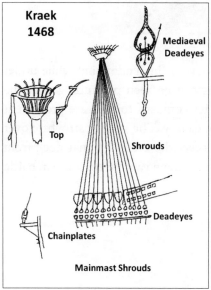

Here we see the stern view of the Tudor ship while under construction. Four guns can be seen protruding over the side, while the two privies (officers' toilets) are prominent on each side of the stern gallery. The strange structure over the upper deck is to protect the crews on that deck from injury, should the massive mizzen yard be cut loose in battle and fall.

drawing by David James

This is the foredeck arrangement. On the upper foredeck can be seen the horizontal windlass used to hoist the massive foresail. Forward of this is a post with sheaves which was part of the pulley system needed to carry out this task. The strange oval opening onto the lower deck was the crew quarters. It gave some shelter from the elements but was far from comfortable or even dry in heavy weather. The heel of the bowsprit projects out of the opening and is secured below the deck planking to a stout timber. The protective awning has not yet been fitted as in the stern view.

Sources: *Archaeology of the Boat*
              Written by Basil Greenhill
              Published by A. & C. Black Publishers

              Model Shipwright
              Written by John Bowen
              Conway Maritime Press

Deck arrangements

Through beams

Few of the images considered have through beams (beams projecting through the side of the ship). It is possible that in practice it had been found difficult to waterproof the joint between beam and hull planking, and beams may have created problems when the ship lay alongside a stone quay. From the images considered, beams were no longer fitted in this manner by the mid-fifteenth century.

Oddly, there are no projecting beams that could be used for catting the anchors. Where fastenings are shown, the anchor is simply tied to the bulwark, as in the carrack of 1475, while the Mataro votive ship model has a sheave in the bulwark rail in the waist of the ship. This would enable the rope from the crown of the anchor to be led to a windlass, enabling the crew to hoist it up the side of the ship and make it secure while at sea. Sandro Botticelli (c. 1445 to 1510) and Vittore Carpaccio (c. 1459) both show cathead beams in their paintings of Mediterranean ships.

Stern galleries

Only six ships have pronounced stern galleries. These are prominent in the 1468 *kraek* and 1475 carrack, while other ships have their quarterdecks ending above the sterns with no projection over the rudder heads. By Henry VIII's time, the tucked sterns had given way to the flat transom. Such transoms were quicker to construct than tucked ones, which was particularly important when more ships were needed to meet imminent invasion. The tucked stern did not vanish, as it can be seen in eighteenth-century ships, mainly to stop water penetrating the end grain of planks and rotting them.

Anchors

Fourteen of the images have anchors; the anchors of the others are not shown due to the angles at which the ships are depicted, and because two are at anchor. The style of anchor is the 'Fisherman', or in later years, the Admiralty pattern. This has a cast shank and arms, with a wooden bar across the upper end to ensure that one palm bit into the sea bed to hold the ship steady.

Awnings and netting

Eight of the images have awnings. The quarterdeck awnings are supported by a pitched roof structure, with the ridge in northern European ships fitted in a fore and aft position. The Mediterranean ships have them athwartships.

Figureheads

These are sometimes vestigial, as seen in the images attributed to Willem A Cruce, and those of the Hastings ship and the 1400 Danzig ship. Henry VIII's ships all have equally small figureheads, while the 1475 carrack, 1468 **kraek**, and the German ships of 1460 all have modestly sized griffin or crocodilian figureheads. Unlike these examples, Michael Stanhope's ship of 1493 has a massive figurehead extending back along the foredeck and pierced with gunports. Another figurehead, portrayed by Hans Holbein in 1530, shows a large, fierce, wolf-like animal with gaping jaws. Since the Tudor coat of arms featured dragons and greyhounds, a greyhound was chosen as a suitable figurehead for the Newport ship model.

Sterns

Contemporary sketches and paintings suggest hulls usually had tucked sterns. However, the Willem A Cruce sketches clearly show transom sterns. Stern galleries appear on some of the larger vessels, with the forerunners of quarter galleries also in evidence (see the 1468 **kraek** and 1475 carrack).

Hulls

Some northern vessels have extremely bluff 'apple-cheeked' bows. Such a hull shape must have been carvel planked, using stealers to drastically reduce the number of planks needed around the sharp curve. Clinker planking does not lend itself to such 'plank loss' measures. The model illustrated in the Newport ship brochure suggests she had a fine entry and run aft, which denotes probable northern rather than southern ancestry.

The Newport ship seems to have been a single-plank clinker build. In comparison, Henry V's *Grace Dieu*, built in Southampton in 1418, had triple-clinker planking. This was found to be increasingly impractical, and the clinker method was discontinued for larger ships, though it survived in smaller wooden boats until the invention of fibreglass hull construction. Hawse holes are in evidence in larger ships, with an occasional cathead beam on southern ships only. The Botticelli and Carpaccio paintings show this.

Deck planking

Only southern ship data is available regarding this. Where seen, deck planking seems to have been extremely wide, with the Mataro ship and Botticelli's work clearly illustrating this. Oddly, Botticelli shows the planks on the quarterdeck going athwartships and not fore and aft as one would expect. Curiously, the deck planking on the Mataro ship's quarterdeck is laid in chevron fashion!

Plank widths

When the Dartmouth ship *Marie Bricxam* (*Marie Brixham*) needed repairs at Bordeaux in 1502, the timber required was ninety-six *taules de carvel* (literally carvel boards). Each board was twenty-six Bordeaux feet long by one foot wide. Over 1,900 feet of planking was replaced in what seems to be a skeleton-built ship. I have included these details to determine the size and availability of timber at the time.

Rudders

These were invariably stern hung, the side rudder having become obsolete at sea, although it survived on Lake Geneva until the nineteenth century. Small rowing boats maintained a steering oar, as clearly illustrated in German ships illustration of 1490. Tillers had a rectangular mortice in the end which fitted over a tenon on the top of a rudder, possibly with a whipstaff, although this is not confirmed in any images, as it would have been hidden below the quarterdeck. The existence of a whipstaff is dictated by the number of decks above the position of the tiller(s). In the nineteenth and early twentieth centuries, Brixham and Lowestoft trawlers had long tillers on deck.

Shroud tensioning devices

Deadeyes were usually a northern device, triangular in shape, as seen in the image of the Danzig ship. The Block and taikle system (handy billy) was usually seen on southern vessels, although both systems are clearly shown on the carrack of 1468. Given the rapid increase in sail size and the massive masts needed to support them, means had to be devised to support the greatly increased deadloads from these, as well as from larger yards and live wind loads. Similarly, these loads needed to be transferred down to deck level by a vast number of shrouds shown on some ships. On larger ships, these tended to number around fourteen to sixteen. Matters seem to have become simpler towards the end of the fifteenth century, with slimmer masts and fewer shrouds.

Masts

All masts seem to have been massively oversized, which may account for the great numbers of shrouds drawn in contemporary sketches. It has also been suggested that some masts were of composite-construction and bound with woldings (ropes wound tightly round the mast components), as indicated on many sketches. Having such massive weight (mast, yard and sailcloth, plus the wind load imposed) so high up must have raised the ship's centre of gravity, which if sited too high would approach the centre of buoyancy and decrease hull stability, even to the point of capsize. Vertical timbers were fitted on the outside of hulls to evenly distribute the upward pull of shrouds across as deep an area as practical on the ship's side. Another function of these timbers was to stiffen the ship to prevent her hogging and sagging in heavy seas. On large ships, they would literally bend when a wave crest was in the middle of the ship, and then sag when wave crests were supporting the bow and stern, with a trough beneath the middle of the ship. For an example, see Carpaccio's work. Additionally, it is worth noting that towering forecastles and aftercastles must have raised a ship's centre of gravity as well as catching the wind, all decreasing stability.

Ships were single masted until the beginning of the fifteenth century, with the mast itself being formed from a single tree trunk of suitable diameter, described as a 'pole mast'. The normal method of fixing it was to step it into a block on the keelson, where it passed through the deck beams (called 'mast partners') and gave some support. Additional support was provided by shrouds attached to the masthead and secured to the ship's sides. These were tightened by lanyards in deadeyes on northern ships, or a block and taikle system on Mediterranean ships.

As vessels grew larger, masts needed to be bigger and longer to carry the larger sails. It isn't known when built-up masts first appeared in northern Europe, but hints appear in documents dated from the mid-fourteenth century. Such masts were built from several pieces of timber scarfed together and secured by iron or rope bands known as woldings, which are often seen in contemporary mediaeval images. In 1348, it was recorded that iron bands were made to fit the mast of King Edward III's ship *Cog Thomas*, a task that employed six carpenters for twenty-one working days. In 1359, four hawsers made of white (untarred) Bridport rope were supplied for knotting about the mast of the Royal ship *Alice*. These were heavy ropes, weighing 256 pounds (116 kg) in total. This suggests the mast was not only built up but was quite large. Woldings were sometimes held in place by cheap clout nails, probably large-headed and used to ensure the rope did not easily slip off when under stress.

Little else is known about built-up masts, and the only evidence unearthed is from the stump of a mast found in a wreck at Woolwich in 1912, with this wreck perhaps being Henry VII's *Sovereign*. The mast was fifty-two inches (1,320 millimetres) in diameter, comprised of a central pine core surrounded by eight oaken baulks, all held together by iron bands. A sketch of the mast can be seen below.

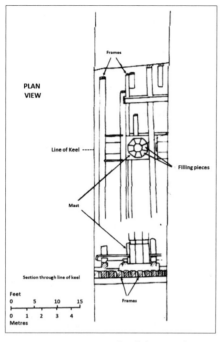

sketch by David James

Masts were often built from the salvaged parts of other masts. For example, in 1416 the great mast of the 1,000-ton *Jesus* was constructed with parts from seventeen other masts. To raise the massive yards, a sheave needed to be fitted into the mast. This enabled the halyard (haulyard) to return to deck level and be attached to a capstan or windlass. The height of such masts is rarely recorded; it has been suggested that *Grace Dieu* of 1418 had a mast that was 190-feet tall. Since her hull length was 125 feet (38.1 metres), contemporary Mediterranean shipwrights would have needed to provide a mast of at least 180 feet (54.9 metres). This height seems to have been confirmed by an Italian galley captain who dined aboard the *Grace Dieu* in 1430.

The Swedish *Stora Kafveln*, a great caravel built 1532, had a length of 126 feet (38.4 metres), beam of thirty-nine feet (11.9 metres), and draught of twenty-one feet (6.5 metres). Her mast was comprised of a central tree that was 114 feet (34.8 metres) in height, the circumference of which was 10.5 feet (3.2 metres). This was secured to four 'filling pieces', each seventy-two feet (twenty-two metres) long.

Shipwrights seemed to use a proportional system to calculate mast height in relation to hull length. The *Regent* of Bristol had:

Bowsprit: eighty-four feet
Foremast: eighty-four feet
Mainmast: 114 feet
Main topmast: eighty-four feet
Mizzenmast: ninety-three feet
Bonaventure mizzenmast: eighty-four feet

Sources: *Cogs, Caravels and Galleons*
Edited by Robert Gardiner & Richard W. Unger
Published by Conway Maritime Press

The Good Ship
Written by Ian Friel
Published by the British Museum Press

Awning supports
The 1475 carrack and the 1468 *kraek* both show massive structures. Given the rapid rise in sail areas, requiring massive masts and yards to support them, ropes of organic materials could well have failed by being too slight, rotting, or fraying after a period at sea. Furthermore, their being damaged by enemy gunfire would cause the heavy timbers to which they were attached to fall catastrophically. So, what was the defence against such a collapse? The tapestry of Willem A Cruce hints that the awning over the aftercastle deck had some form of roof; and southern European ships had the ridges of these aftercastles athwartships, while in northern versions the ridges were fore and aft. Carpaccio and Botticelli's works both portray more modest netting supports.

Parrel trucks

Parrels secured yards to masts, enabling the yard to be pulled up and down the mast with minimum friction. They also enabled the yard to be pivoted round in the horizontal plane to make best use of available winds. A taikle was used to slacken the parrel when it was being moved, and once in the required position it was tightened against the mast. Large ships such as the carrack of 1475 and the *kraek* of 1468 show three, four and five parrel trucks, while sketch WA 206 shows only one, as does the Michael Stanhope ship.

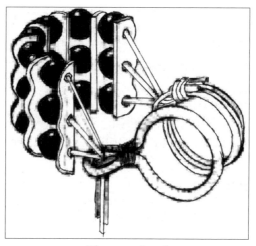

Three parrel truck

Mainsails with bonnets

All ships carry square sails on mainmasts, foremasts and topmasts, with a lateen-rigged sail on mizzen and bonaventure masts. Bonnets were simply laced onto the lower edge of a sail to increase its area. Gentile de Fabriano's painting of a ship below shows a bonnet ripping off in a squall. Top sails, where hoisted, were either sheeted into the top (Italian carrack 1470-80 and Carpaccio detail, however WA shows the topsail sheets belayed to mainyard)

Gentile de Fabriano images; Malaga ship; W A sketches

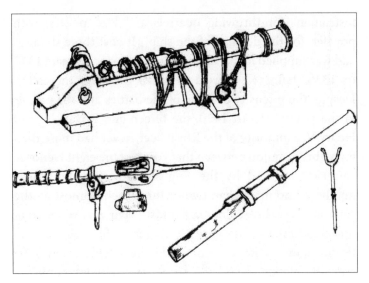

Armament

The image above shows:

(a) A large cannon, possibly serpentine, mounted on a wooden block. The breech block is wedged in place and ready for firing.

(b) A falconet light cannon, with the breech block alongside. The tapered section of the block matches a taper in the barrel, while small holes at the rear of the block chamber indicate where the locking wedge fits. This type of swivel gun could be mounted anywhere on the ship, even in the tops. This weapon was also known as a 'murderer'.

(c) *Couleuvrines à main* (handguns), a simple sort of gun that could be fired through holes in the ship's bulwarks.

The advent of cannon in the fourteenth century had very little, if any, immediate impact on the nature of sea warfare. The earliest known naval cannon was "a certain iron instrument for throwing quarrels and lead pellets, with powder, for the defence of the ship". It cost three shillings and was supplied for an English Royal ship in the years 1337 to 1338. Guns were used in small numbers thereafter. Despite the intensity of some of the battles and sea patrols in the years 1415 to 1420, the fifteen-gun Royal ships of Henry V, a minority of the Royal fleet, never had more than forty-three cannon between them. Five of the eight Genoese carracks captured by the English had guns, but these numbered no more than two or three each. Almost all the cannon were breechloading, most having two separate breech chambers. This gave a faster rate of fire than muzzle-loading guns, as they did not need to be pulled back into the hull for reloading, and the spare breech block could be reloaded while the gun was being aimed and fired.

Stone round shot discovered on the Newport ship suggest she may have been armed or transporting ammunition for other warships. As canon were relatively new and prestigious, the guns, stone round shot and black powder would all be quite costly, and therefore fitted only in large ships with valuable cargoes or important passengers and crew.

The earliest clearly identifiable gunports on ship sides can be seen in the manuscript of Louis de Bruges, Lord of Gruythuse, dated 1482; Michael Stanhope's seal of 1493; and the Ark in *Weltchronik* (*World History*), 1493. These examples seem to predate the traditional date of the gunport's invention by the Frenchman François Descharges in 1501. Regardless, until the invention of the gunport, guns were mounted to fire over the gunwale in the waist, with smaller ones being placed in the forecastles and aftercastles, and a few in the fighting tops. For examples, see the *kraek* of 1468 and carrack of 1475. It is worth noting that gunports and sally ports of this time do not seem to have possessed port lids.

Guns of the period were unhandy and difficult to aim, slow to reload (although the breechloading guns were faster than the muzzle-loaded guns of the day), and possibly as dangerous to the gunners as those they were shooting at. The poor metallurgical skills and techniques used to cast guns of the time meant that it was not uncommon for the guns themselves to explode, though this does not reflect on the skill of the foundry workers. It merely means that, as with all new ideas, there was a development period that presented unforeseen problems to which solutions had to be sought.

Gunports tended to weaken clinker-built ships drastically, but this problem did not arise with frame-built ships, as their frames could be placed to suit the cutting of ports without reducing strength. Gunport lids can be seen on the *Mary Rose* and *Henri Grace a Dieu* ships. Long iron darts, called 'gads' by the English, are shown in the tops, ready to be hurled into the enemy ship below. Other weapons used included crossbows and small swivel guns. Ammunition was hoisted up to the top by a crane, and some images show bags of ammunition being hoisted aloft using the craneline.

Sources: *Cogs, Caravels and Galleons*
Edited by Robert Gardiner & Richard W. Unger
Published by Conway Maritime Press

Sailing Ships of War, 1400-1860
Written by Frank Howard
Published by Conway Maritime Press

Culverin (*couleuvrine*)

These weapons originated in Germany and are first mentioned in Burgundian documents at the Siege of Compiegne in 1430. Duke Phillip of Burgundy bought some from German foundries and hired German gunners to operate them. The barrel length varied from two feet (600 millimetres) to four feet (1200 millimetres), with a calibre of two inches (fifty millimetres), either in one piece or with separate breech blocks. Each breechloading gun came with three or four separate breech blocks.

One surviving culverin shot lead balls that were one and a half inches (forty millimetres) in diameter and weighed 12.2 ounces (360 grams), while another fired two-inch (fifty-millimetre) lead shot weighing 24.69 ounces (700 grams). The guns were stocked in wood, with the larger ones on trestles, while the smaller ones could be held in the gunner's hand or more frequently mounted on ribauldequins. Charles the Bold of Burgundy's heavier culverins had hooks on the barrel ends (*couleuvrine à croc*) to absorb recoil when fired from ramparts. Later, these evolved into arquebuses.

Serpentines

These ideal field guns appeared about 1430 and were more powerful than the culverins. They were mobile weapons mounted on carriages with large-diameter, iron-shod wheels. They often had elevating devices and were usually breechloading. In length they were three and a half feet (1,050 millimetres) to seven feet (2,100 millimetres) long, with calibres varying between two inches (fifty millimetres) and six inches (150 millimetres)

Couleuvrines à main (handguns)

Not to be confused with true culverins, this mediaeval handgun is the forerunner of the musket and the rifle. It was infrequent before 1360, but by 1411 Duke John the Good of Burgundy had over 4,000. His successor, Charles the Bold, equipped one third of his infantry with them. One fifteenth-century gun in Nuremberg had a barrel one foot and three inches (375 millimetres) long with a bore of about three quarters of an inch (twenty-one millimetres). It had a short squat barrel attached to a long stave which the gunner held under one arm while he applied the smouldering match to the venthole. At the beginning of the fifteenth century, this erratic mini cannon was improved by two innovations: the shoulder stock and the serpentine lock. These enabled a soldier to aim the weapon without having to concentrate on putting the smouldering match against the venthole of the gun.

The shot was either lead or cast-iron, with iron being the shot of choice as it pierced armour more effectively than lead. Tests on a replica fifteenth-century handgun proved that iron shot could pierce one tenth of an inch of mild steel plate, while lead shot performed less well. Masons would cut stones into spheres for larger bored guns, taking about half a day to make one shot, using a board with a hole in it to gauge that the shot was of the correct diameter

Sources: *Armies of Mediaeval Burgundy, 1364-1477*
            Written by Nicholas Michael
            Published by Osprey Publishing

The completed model

Below can be seen two images of the completed model of the Newport ship. The first is a view of the starboard quarter, while the second shows the seizing grapnel suspended off the bowspirit; as well as her greyhound figurehead, and the strengthening of the timbers amidships, fixed to those running along the sides of the ship. This model is on permanent public display in Pembroke Museum, the Town Hall, Main Street, Pemproke.

photo and model by David James

The completed model showing the seizing grapnel suspended off the bowsprit, the greyhound figurehead and the strengthening timbers amidships, fixed to those running along the sides of the ship.
This ship is on permanent public display in Pembroke Museum, the Town Hall, Main Street, Pembroke

photo and model by David James

Appendices

The comparison table below is based on the images featured throughout this work, with hull ratios taken from the Timbotta manuscript and the British Library's Cotton manuscripts of 1455 (British Library, Cotton manuscript Titus A XXVI).

Tons	Keel/beam ratio	Beam/depth ratio
625	2.50;1	2.83;1
437.5	2.59;1	2.55;1
437.5	2.50;1	
312.5	2.90;1	2.27;1
187.5	2.78;1	3.00;1
156.5	2.93;1	2.41;1
125	3.33;1	

Table of dimensions for two ships in the Timbotta manuscript

Tons	Keel Feet/ metres	Beam Feet/ metres	Stem height feet/ metres	Stern height feet/ metres	Depth in hold feet/ metres
625	96.5	38.6	51.7	39.7	13.6
	29.4	11.8	15.8	12.1	4.1
437.5	82.3	31.7	40.9	23.8	12.5
	25.1	9.7	12.5	7.3	3.8

Tables of dimensions for earlier vessels from 1000 AD to 1305 AD

Ship	Date	Length	Breadth	L/B ratio
Skuldelev warship	1000 AD	18.00m	2.5m	7:1
Skuldelev Knarr	1000AD	13.5m	3.2m	4.2:1
Skuldelev Knarr	1000 AD	16.5m	4.6m	3.5:1
Skuldelev Knarr	1000 AD	12.0m	2.5m	4.8:1
Dover ship	1305 AD	20.0m	5.5m	3.6:1
Kalmar boat	1250AD	11.2m	4.6m	2.4:1
Bergen Ship	1250AD	25.9m	9.14m	2.8:1

Sources: *'Longships, Knarrs and Cogs'*
Written by Roald Morcken
Published in *The Mariner's Mirror*, vol. 74 (4)

Cargo capacity of Viking ships

	Gokstad ship	Long Serpent
Length	23.24m	59.7m
Beam	5.20m	13.4m
Depth	1.60m	4.1m
Tonnage	40 lasts	683 lasts

Sources: *'Longships, Knarrs and Cogs'*
Written by Roald Morcken
Published in *The Mariner's Mirror*, vol. 74 (4)

English ships hired by the Crown from 1449 to 1451

200 tons and over			*100-199 tons*			*Under 100 tons*		
1 ships of 400 tons			4 ships of 180 tons			3 ships of 90 tons		
1	"	350 "	2	"	170 "	11	"	80 "
5	"	300 "	7	"	160 "	1	"	75 "
1	"	290 "	4	"	140 "	10	"	70 "
1	"	270 "	2	"	130 "	1	"	68 "
3	"	260 "	11	"	120 "	1	"	65 "
6	"	240 "	5	"	110 "	15	"	60 "
1	"	230 "	9	"	100 "	2	"	58 "
5	"	220 "				1	"	57 "
10	"	200 "				1	"	55 "
						10	"	50 "
						1	"	45 "
						17	"	40 "
						2	"	36 "
						2	"	30 "
						1	"	12 "

Total ships 34 **Total ships 44** **Total ships 83**

Foreign ships hired by the Crown from 1449 to 1451
The figures below are taken from foreign accounts.

200 tons and over	*100-199 tons*	*Under 100 tons*	
2 ships of 200 tons	1 ship of 160 tons	1 ship of 90 tons	
	1 " 140 "	4 " 80 "	
		5 " 60 "	
		1 " 55 "	
		1 " 50 "	
		1 " 45 "	
		5 " 40 "	
		1 " 36 "	
		2 " 30 "	
		4 " 25 "	
Total ships 1	*Total ships 2*	*Total ships 27*	

English ships granted safe conducts and trading licences from 1472 to 1483

200 tons and over	*100-199 tons*	*Under 200 tons*	
2 Ships of 450 tons	2 ships of 180 tons	2 ships of 90 tons	
3 " 400 "	7 " 160 "	7 " 80 "	
3 " 300 "	1 " 140 "	2 " 70 "	
3 " 280 "	5 " 120 "	6 " 60 "	
3 " 250 "	6 " 100 "	4 " 50 "	
1 " 240 "		1 " 40 "	
5 " 200 "		1 " 24 "	
Total ships 21	*Total ships 17*	*Total ships 23*	

Northern French ships

200 tons and over	*100-199 tons*	*Under 100 tons*
1 ship of 200 tons	2 ships of 160 tons	2 ships of 90 tons
	1 " 130 "	2 " 80 "
	4 " 120 "	8 " 70 "
	13 " 100 "	18 " 60 "
		1 " 50 "
		7 " 40 "
		1 " 35 "
		2 " 30 "
		1 " 24 "
		1 " 20 "
Total ships 1	*Total ships 20*	*Total ships 43*

Southern French ships

200 tons and over	*100-199 tons*	*Under 100 tons*
2 ships of 800 tons	3 ships of 180 tons	Nil
1 " 600 "	2 " 160 "	
	2 " 150 "	
	2 " 140 "	
	6 " 120 "	
	3 " 110 "	
	2 " 105 "	
	7 " 100 "	
Total ships 1	*Total ships 27*	*Total ships*

Breton ships

200 tons and over			*100-199 tons*			*Under 100 tons*		
1 ship of 1000 tons			1 ship of 162 tons			2 ships of 95 tons		
3	"	800 "	4	"	160 "	3	"	90 "
1	"	350 "	2	"	140 "	13	"	80 "
1	"	250 "	2	"	130 "	3	"	70 "
4	"	250 "	13	"	120 "	11	"	60 "
4	"	200 "	3	"	110 "	1	"	51 "
			1	"	106 "	1	"	50 "
			30	"	100 "	1	"	44 "
						2	"	40 "
Total ships 10			*Total ships 56*			*Total ships 37*		

Northern rigging comparison table

A question mark in the tables hereafter refers to an uncertainty in the source material. For example, the 1468 *kraek* tapestry shows no clear indication of parrels, martlets, tops, or seizing grapnels.

Ship	Shrouds mainmast	Deadeyes lanyards	Parrel size
Carrack 1475	16/side	Deadeyes & blocks 12 & 4	4 truck main 3 mizz'
Kraek 1468	14/side	deadeyes	Five truck
Kraek tapestry	6	deadeyes	?
English 1426	4	?	?
Hotel Jacques Bourges ship 1445	8	yes	?
Hastings 15th C	4	?	?
Danzig ship 1400	3?	deadeyes	1 truck?
WA 208	7	deadeyes	?
WA 206	5	?	1 truck
WA 207	?	?	?
Stanhope seal 1493	4	deadeyes	1 truck
Seal Louis de Bourbon 1463-86	?	?	?
John Holland	?	?	?
German ships 1490 history of seafaring	7	deadeyes	3 truck
Kings Lynn pew	5	?	?
Earl of Warwick 1485	5?	?	?
The Ark Weldkronic 1493	no	no	no

Martlets	Guns	Masts	Tops	Ratlines	Seizing grapnels
Mainyard & mizzen	3 Q deck/ one in mizzen top	3	3	yes	yes
Mainyard & mizzen	5 Q deck one in top	3	3	No- Ladder up mast	yes
?	5 in after castle	3	?	yes	?
no	0	1	1	no	no
yes	6	3	1	yes	?
no	no	3	1	yes	no
no	no	1	1	yes	?
yes	?	4	1	yes	no
no	2	3	1	Yes	?
yes	?	2	1	Yes	no
no	12 in gun ports	4	4	yes	no
?	?	3	1	no	no
?	no	1	1	?	?
No	2 ??	3	1	yes	yes
no	no	2	2	yes	?
?	3	4	1	?	n/a
no	4 ports cut	no	no	no	n/a

Ship	Shrouds mainmast	Deadeyes lanyards	Parrel size
Santa Catarina do Monte Sinai	10	?	3 truck
1482 MSS Louis de Bruges	?	?	?
Passages outré Mer, late 15th C	5 shrouds 5 backstay	?	?
Dutch Carvel 15th c	4	?	?
Holbein 1530	6	deadeyes	3 truck
Henry Grace a Dieu	?	?	?
Mary Rose	7	?	?
Jesus of Lubeck	?	?	?
Grand Mistress	?	?	?

Northern yards were usually one piece, except in the case of the carrack of 1475 and *Santa Catarina do Monte Sinai*, which each show two-piece yards.

Martlets	Guns	Masts	Tops	Ratlines	Seizing grapnels
no	numerous	3	2	yes	?
No	6 in ports	3	1	yes	?
no	None ?	1	1	yes	yes
no	3 round ports	2	no	yes	no
no	One lidded port	3	3	yes	?
?	Yes, in lidded ports	4	8	no	Yes + yard hooks
no	Yes in lidded ports	4	4	yes	Yes + hooks On yards
?	ditto	4	4	?	Hooks on yards
no	ditto	4	3?	?	no

Northern hull comparison table

Ship	Clinker	Sally port	Thro' beams	Barrels
Carrack 1475	no	no	No	1
Kraek 1468		yes	No	1
Kraek tapestry	no	yes	no	no
English 1426	?	yes	no	no
Ship Hotel Jacques Bourges	yes	no	no	no
Hastings 15th C	?	no	No	Leadline in use
Danzig ship 1400	yes	no	no	no
WA 208	no	no	no	No
WA 206	no	?	no	leadline stbd Quarter
WA 207	no	?	?	no
Ark 1493	no	no	no	no
Stanhope seal	no	no	no	no
Seal Louis de Bourbon 1463–86	yes	no	no	No
John Holland	Hulk clinker	no	?	no
German ships 1490 History of seafaring	Hulk derivative	no	no	no
Kings Lynn pew	Uncertain	no	no	no
Earl of Warwick sketch 1485	possible	no	no	no

Vertical strakes	Stern gallery	Anchor	Awnings/nettings	Horizontal wales	Figurehead
5	yes	Grapnel & fisherman	Wood & net	4	Griffin/Crocodile
5	yes	no	wood	4	Griffin/crocodile
5	yes	no	wood	4	Griffin/crocodile
no	no	no	No	no	No
no	yes	no	?	4	?
?	no	yes	no	?	Hint of crocodile
11	no	yes	No	2	Small
no	no	no	nets	4	No
No	?	yes	?	3	Hint of one
*	no	?	?	2	No
3	yes	no	?	3	no
no	?	Fisherman	no	no	Large Dragon/crocodile
yes	no	Fisherman	no	No	No
no	no	no	no	no	no
Yes	no	2 fisherman	No	yes	griffin Crocodile
no	no	?	no	no	?
yes	no	?	yes	yes	indistinct

Ship	Clinker	Sally port	Thro' beams	Barrels
Santa Catarina do Monte Sinai	Not clear	no	no	no
1482 MSS Louis de Bruges	Not clear	no	no	no
Passages outré Mer, late 15th C	no	no	no	no
Dutch carvel 15th c	no	no	no	3 sideways-fenders?
Holbein 1530	no	no	no	no
Henry Grace a Dieu	?	no	no	no
Mary Rose	yes	no	no	no
Jesus of Lubeck	?	no	no	no
Grand Mistress	?	no	no	no

* vertical strakes suggested.

The Michael Stanhope, John Holland and Louis de Bourbon seals clearly show coats of arms on mainsails.

Vertical strakes	Stern gallery	Anchor	Awnings/ nettings	Horizontal wales	Figurehead
no	no	fisherman	yes	no	----
Upper-works only	no	fisherman	no	Yes	?
numerous	yes	Fisherman	no	no	no
no	no	no	yes	3	no
4	no	Fisherman	no	1	Large dog like
no	Flat transom	fisherman	?	?	vestigial
no	Flat transom	fisherman	yes	no	vestigial
no	Flat transom	anchored	no	no	?
no	Flat transom	fisherman	no	no	no

Southern European ship rigging details

Ship	Shrouds Mainmast	Deadeyes lanyards	Parrel Size	Martlets
Timbotta 1445	9	deadeyes	?	?
Italian engraving 1470-80	?	?	?	?
Sandro Botticelli 1445-1510	?	?	?	?
Italian Carrack 1470-80	10	?	?	?
Mataro ship Mid 15th C	3	Lanyards & blocks	3 truck	?
Pizigano 15th C Image 194	?	?	?	?
Gentile de Fabriano 15th C Stern image	4	?	No parrel shown	yes
Malaga ship Early 15th C	11 painting 5 on drawing	blocks	3 truck	no
Carpaccio Detail 203	8	?	?	?
Carpaccio Detail 204	12	?	?	yes
Santa Maria Replica 1492	12	blocks	?	no
Carpaccio painting 1459	6	blocks	?	no
Venetian galleasse 1486	5	blocks	3 truck?	no

Guns	Masts	Tops	Tops	Yards
no	1	1	Mast ladder	?
No	3	?	?	?
No	3	1	?	1 piece
no	3	2	No	1 piece
No	1	1	no	1 piece
no	2	1	?	?
no	2	1	Mast ladder	2 piece
no	3	1	Mast ladder	2 piece
No	3	1	Mast ladder	?
No	3	1	ratlines	2 piece
?	3	1	yes	2 piece
no	3	1	no	2 piece
no	2	1	?	2 piece

Southern European hull details

Ship	Clinker	Sally port	Thro' beams	Barrels	Vertical strakes
Timbotta 1445	?	?	no	no	8
Italian Engraving 1470/80	?	no	no	no	13
Sandro Botticelli 1445–1510	?	?	cathead	no	?
Italian Carrack 1470–80	no	no	no	no	14
Mataro Ship Mid 15th C	no	no	18 On two levels	no	4
Pizigano Mid 15th C Image 194	?	no	no	no	?
Gentile de Fabriano Mid 15th C	no	no	no	no	5
Malaga Early 15th C	?	no	20 Two levels See sketch	no	4
Carpaccio Detail 203	?	no	?	no	8
Carpaccio Detail 204	?	no	?	no	no
Santa Maria replica 1492	no	no	no	no	10
Carpaccio Painting 1459	no	no	cathead	no	5
Livro das Armadas Lisbon 1500 Numerous ships on painting	no	?	unclear	no	Artist hints at beams
Venetian galleasse	?	no	no	no	no

Stern gallery	Anchor	Awnings/nettings	Guns	Horizontal wales	Figurehead	Seizing grapnels
no	no	no	no	7	Small stump	no
no	no	no	no	4	?	no
no	?	Yes Aft of main mast	no	?	?	?
?	no	yes	No	5	no	?
no	no	no	no	4	Small stump	no
no	no	no	no	?	no	No
no	grapnel	no	no	5	no	no
no	fisherman	no	4	4	?	no
yes	fisherman	?	?	6	no	No
yes	?	yes	Ports visible	6 ?	no	no
no	?	no	2?	6	no	no
no	fisherman	yes	no	5 & 8	no	?
no	fisherman	yes	no	5 & 8	no	?
3 sterns shown – no galleries	?	no	Ports suggested	Numbers not clear	Not enough detail	?
yes	fisherman	Poop only	no	no	Pointed ram	no

Bibliography

A History of Seafaring
Written by George Bass
Published by Walker

An Illustrated History of the Royal Navy
Written by John Winton
Published by Salamander Books

Archaeologia Cambrensis, LXXVII (1922)
Written by Wilfrid J. Hemp, FSA
Published by Cambrian Archaeological Association

Archaeology of the Boat
Written by Basil Greenhill
Published by A. & C. Black Publishers

Armies of Mediaeval Burgundy, 1364-1477
Written by Nicholas Michael
Published by Osprey Publishing

Llibre del Consolat y dels Fets Maritims
Written by Valencian legislators

Boutell's Heraldry
Written by Charles Boutell
Published by F. Warne Publishers

Cogs, Caravels and Galleons
Edited by Robert Gardiner & Richard W. Unger
Published by Conway Maritime Press

Collection of Ship Models
Published by National Maritime Museum, Greenwich

Dictionary of Ship Types
Written by Alfred Dudzus & Ernst Henriot
Published by Conway Maritime Press

Die Entwiklung der Wichtigsten Schiffstypen
Written by Bernhard Hagedorn
Published by Karl Curtius

English Merchant Shipping, 1460 to 1540
Written by Dorothy Burwash
Published by University of Toronto Press

Hampshire and Isle of Wight Directory
Written by William White
Published by Robert Leader

John Talbot and the War in France, 1427-1453
Written by by A. J. Pollard
Published by Pen & Sword Military

'Longships, Knarrs and Cogs'
Written by Roald Morcken
Published in The Mariner's Mirror, vol. 74 (4)

Model Shipwright
Written by John Bowen
Conway Maritime Press

Newport Medieval Ship, A Guide
Edited by Bob Trett
Published by the Friends of the Newport Ship

Peregrinatio in Terram Sanctam
Written by Bernhard von Breydenbach
Published by Peter Schöffer the Elder

Sailing Ships
Written by Bjorn Landstrom
Published by Allen & Unwin

Sailing Ships of War, 1400-1860
Written by Frank Howard
Published by Conway Maritime Press

Schedelsche Weltchronik
Written by Hatmann Schedel
Published by Anton Koberger

The Galleon
Written by Peter Kirsch
Published by Conway Maritime Press

The Good Ship
Written by Ian Friel
Published by the British Museum Press

The Ship in the Mediaeval Economy, 600-1600
Written by Richard W. Unger
Published by McGill-Queen's University Press

Assorted Images

Anthony Anthony

Anthony Anthony, an artillery officer, described and drew the fleet of King Henry VIII in the *Anthony Roll*. Above can be seen his *Henri Grace a Dieu*, completed and commissioned in 1514. Attack grapnels are clearly seen on the bowsprit ends, as well as seizing grapnels on the yard ends.

Mary Rose

The *Mary Rose* was built in Portsmouth between 1509 and1511. She sank off Southsea Castle on 19 July 1545

Anthony Roll

The carrack *Jesus of Lubeck*, again from the *Anthony Roll*. She was a 600-ton ship with a superstructure typical of the early sixteenth century. King Henry VIII had purchased the ship from the Hanseatic League in 1544 and armed her with two bronze cannons, two bronze culverins, and two bronze sakers. She also bore forged iron breech loaders, four port pieces, ten serpentines, four fowlers, twelve bases, two top guns (mounted in the masthead tops), and twenty each of revolving case shot and handguns. No gunport lids are visible.

Another of the *Anthony Roll* ships, *The Grand Mistress*, of 450 tons

Index

Ship names in italics

A Ship of King Henry VII – 1490 AD

Ye Mary Fortune